Wild*f*lowers of Ohio

rs of Ohio

Robert L. Henn

Indiana University Press

BLOOMINGTON AND INDIANAPOLIS

Publication of this book is made possible in part with the assistance of a Challenge Grant from the National Endowment for the Humanities, a federal agency that supports research, education, and public programming in the humanities.

MANUFACTURED IN THE UNITED STATES OF AMERICA

Library of Congress Cataloging-in-Publication Data

Henn, Robert L., date
 Wildflowers of Ohio / Robert L. Henn.
  p. cm.
 Includes bibliographical references (p.) and index.
 ISBN 0-253-33369-5 (cloth : alk. paper). — ISBN 0-253-21167-0 (pbk. : alk. paper)
  1. Wild flowers—Ohio—Identification. 2. Wild flowers—Ohio—Pictorial works. I. Title
 QK180.H45 1998
 582.13'09771—dc21   97-29108

1 2 3 4 5 03 02 01 00 99 98

TO MARGE

CONTENTS

PREFACE

As a boy, I always enjoyed going on field trips with naturalists. I always stayed up close to the naturalist so that I wouldn't miss a single word as he pointed out the importance of all living things in the principle of Biological Diversity. On one of those field trips the naturalist, whose name has long been forgotten, stopped the group near a solitary wildflower growing beside the trail. He pointed out that this beautiful wildflower was the only one of its kind known to be growing in the entire area. After answering several questions about that magnificent specimen, the naturalist continued to lead the group further ahead on the trail. As often happens on field trips, one of the boys lagged far behind the group and had missed the entire experience around the endangered wildflower. Suddenly, that same boy came running up the trail, pushing his way past the group, and went straight up to the naturalist. There he stood, with that same solitary wildflower grasped tightly in his fist, and breathlessly gasped: "What's the name of this flower?"

Needless to say, the naturalist was horrified. After composing himself, the naturalist gave us an unforgettable lesson on the role of wildflowers in the balance of nature, and on the importance of protecting endangered species.

From that experience I learned two lessons: First, for most people who walk the trails, the most often asked question is, "What's the name of this wildflower?" Second, it *is possible* that the specimen in front of you could be the very last one of its kind remaining on the Earth. Extinction means forever.

I hope that this book helps all those who walk the trails to learn the names of the wildflowers, and to protect them in order that people for years to come may enjoy their beauty.

SPONSORS

The publication of this book was made possible by financial contributions from the following organizations and individuals:

Canterbury Garden Club
Janet L. Eby
Melvin H. Fine
Donald R. Geiger
Robert L. Henn
Native Plant Society of the Miami Valley
Carl Noffsinger
Robert W. Smith
Violet R. Strahler
John Trigg
Trotwood Garden Club
Woolpert Consultants

ACKNOWLEDGMENTS

This book could not possibly have been written without the help of many people. I am deeply grateful for the valuable assistance and advice so generously given by Jim Amon, Beavercreek Wetlands; June Barr, Trotwood-Madison High School; Robert A. Briggs; Debbie Brill, Brukner Nature Center; Gary Coovert, Dayton Museum of Natural History; Allison W. Cusick, ODNR Division of Natural Areas and Preserves; Bill Denlinger; Guy L. Denny, ODNR Division of Natural Areas and Preserves; Roberta L. Diehl, Indiana University Press; Charlene Dillon, Miami Valley Native Plant Society; David Dister, Miami Valley Native Plant Society; William B. Elliott; Charles B. Earnhart; Mel Fine, Wegerzyn Horticultural Center; Jane Forsyth, Bowling Green State University; John Gallman, Indiana University Press; Susan Havlish, Indiana University Press; Ken Hays, Centerville High School; Joan Heidelberg, Brukner Nature Center; Dave Henn, Graphic Designs; Melissa K. Hill; Tom Hissong, Aullwood Audubon Center and Farm; Paul E. Knoop, Jr., Natural Areas Consultant; Charity Krueger, Aullwood Audubon Center and Farm; E. J. Koestner, Dayton Museum of Natural History; Al McCabe, Sycamore State Park; Karen McDaniel, Dayton and Montgomery County Public Library; George and Donnalea Phinney; Jo Ann Rose, Fairborn High School; Myron Shank; Jim Stahl, Columbus Metro Parks; Violet R. Strahler; John Trigg, Sinclair Community College; Martin Trent, Sinclair Community College; Cindy Tucci, Brookville High School; Michael Vincent, Miami University; John Walker, Sinclair Community College; Clyde and Jeanne Willis, Otterbein College; and John Woodruff, Illustrations.

PHOTO CREDITS

Most of the photographs were taken by the author. In addition, the author gratefully acknowledges the following people for the contribution of their photographs.

Bill Denlinger: Snow Trillium.

David Dister: Canada Lily, White Baneberry, Indian Cucumber-root, Meadowsweet, Pickerel Weed, Pink Lady's-slipper, Spotted Wintergreen, Virgin's Bower.

Ken Hays: Dwarf Iris, Showy Orchis, Squawroot, Trailing Arbutus, Wild Hyacinth.

Tom Hissong: Skunk Cabbage.

George and Donnalea Phinney: Green Dragon, Fringed Gentian, Fringed Polygala.

Cindy Tucci: Chicory, Day-lily, Crested Dwarf Iris, Foxglove Beardtongue, Hairy Beardtongue, Jack-in-the-Pulpit, Northern Monkshood, Yellow Lady's-slipper, Yellow Salsify.

Jeanne Willis: Blue-eyed Grass, Coltsfoot, Royal Catchfly, Mouse-ear Chickweed, Fireweed, Fragrant Water-lily, Showy Lady's-slipper, Sharp-winged Monkey Flower, Mayapple, Miami-mist, Large Twayblade, Mountain Laurel.

INTRODUCTION

This book is a "user-friendly" guide to the beautiful wildflowers of Ohio. It is designed to be a simple guide to the identification of Ohio's most common species of wildflowers. The photographs of the wildflowers are arranged by color: white, yellow and orange, red and pink, blue and purple, green and brown.

Follow these suggestions when identifying a wildflower. Look at several flowers in front of you. Then visually select an individual that appears to be most "typical" of the plant. Read the entire description of the wildflower that accompanies the photograph. Often, the appearance of the leaves or stem are as important as the flower in its identification. Be sure the wildflower fits all of the description including the time of year. For instance, in April you may see a yellow, daisy-like wildflower, ½" wide, with alternate leaves. However, when you notice in the description that this flower blooms in August–September, then you know the description does not fit a spring wildflower, and thus you must look further. On occasion you may find a wildflower that is not included in this guide. For additional information, refer to the Bibliography.

Remember that wildflowers are only a small part of the whole environment. Trees, insects, birds, and humans are interdependent for their survival. Wildflowers that were once common in many parts of Ohio are becoming rare and limited in their distribution. This has come about because of habitat destruction resulting from intensive farming, use of herbicides, road building, and construction of homes and factories. Indiscriminate picking has also contributed to the decline of many of Ohio's beautiful wildflowers. The Ohio Endangered Plant Law (O.R.C. 1518) designates and protects Ohio's threatened and endangered wildflowers. The picking and digging of wildflowers on state-owned land is prohibited by law.

Carolus Linnaeus (1707-1778), the Swedish botanist, is recognized as the father of modern classification. In 1753, he published *Species Plantarum*, in which he developed the binomial (two-name) system to give each plant a scientific name. In *Wildflowers of Ohio* the scientific names used are from the Second Edition of the *Manual of Vascular Plants of Northeastern United States and Adjacent Canada* by Henry A. Gleason and Arthur Cronquist (1991).

The purpose of this book is to provide a means for the readers to identify, appreciate, and cultivate attitudes toward the conservation of wildflowers as one of Ohio's most valuable natural resources. It is not the intention of the author to offer any medicinal or edible uses of any plants described herein. All such references are included only as a matter of historical interest. Any such use by a reader would be at that reader's own risk.

Enjoy the beautiful wildflowers. Take photographs and memories. Let them live to return next year for others to enjoy.

PARTS OF A FLOWER

A GENERALIZED FLOWER

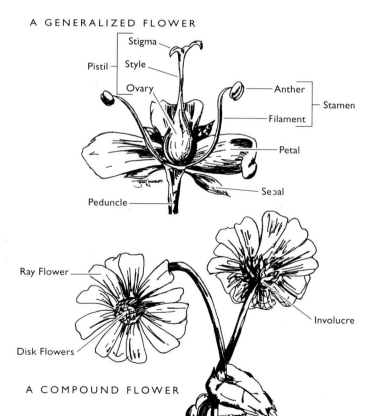

Pistil
Stigma
Style
Ovary

Anther
Stamen
Filament

Petal

Sepal

Peduncle

Ray Flower

Disk Flowers

Involucre

A COMPOUND FLOWER

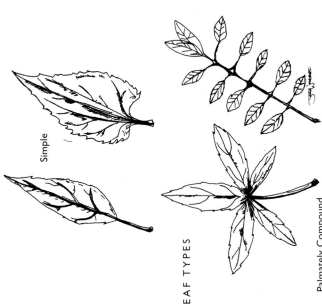

Simple

Pinnately Compound

Palmately Compound

LEAF TYPES

Opposite

Alternate

Whorled

LEAF ARRANGEMENTS

xvi

GLOSSARY

Alternate: Not opposite each other on a stem.

Anther: The enlarged part of the stamen that produces pollen.

Annual: A plant that completes its life cycle and lives for only one growing season.

Axil: The upper angle formed between the leaf and the stem.

Axillary: In the axil.

Biennial: A plant that requires two growing seasons to complete its life cycle, then dies.

Blade: The flat portion of a leaf.

Bract: A small or modified leaf, growing at the base of a single flower or an inflorescence.

Calcareous: Soil rich in lime.

Calyx: A complete set of sepals, the outermost parts of a flower.

Clasping: The base of a leaf that partially surrounds the stem.

Cleft: Deeply cut.

Cleistogamous: A flower which does not open and usually self-pollinates.

Corolla: A complete set of petals in a flower.

Creeping: Describes a stem running along the ground, rooting as it goes.

Disk: In Asteraceae, the central part of the flowering head; it is made up of numerous tiny, tubular disk flowers, usually surrounded by ray flowers.

Divided: Leaf composed of numerous smaller leaflets.

Downy: Covered with very fine, soft hairs.

Ecosystem: The interacting groups of plants and animals and their physical environment which affects them.

Endangered Species: A native Ohio plant species whose natural populations in the state are limited to three or fewer occurrences.

Entire: The margin (edge) of a leaf that is unbroken by teeth, lobes or divisions.

Ephemeral: Spring plants that bloom only for a short period of time.

Filament: The stalk of the stamen which supports the anther.

Glabrous: Without hairs.

Gland: A small structure that secretes oils and sticky substances.

Globose: Sphere-shaped.

Habitat: The place or part of an ecosystem occupied by a plant.

Head: A dense cluster of flowers at the end of a stalk, as in a sunflower.

Inflorescence: A flower-cluster.

Irregular: Describes flowers which are not symmetrical.

Lanceolate: Leaf shaped like a lance, or sword, with pointed tip; several times longer than wide.

Leaflet: One of the blades of a compound leaf.

Linear: Leaf long and narrow with nearly parallel veins and margins.

Lobed: Leaf deeply indented with segments.

Margin: The outside edge of a leaf.

Midrib: The central vein or "rib" of a leaf.

Native: Plants originating in North America, including Ohio.

Naturalized: Plants originally coming from another area but now thoroughly established.

Nerve: A prominent vein of a leaf or petal.

Node: The point on a stem where leaves are borne.

Oblong: Longer than wide.

Opposite: Arranged in pairs on a stem.

Oval: Broadly elliptical, and rounded at the ends.

Ovary: The enlarged base of the pistil that produces seeds.

Palmate: A compound leaf with leaflets radiating from a central point (as fingers from a palm).

Pedicel: The stalk of an individual flower that is part of an inflorescence.

Peduncle: The stalk of a solitary flower or the main stalk of an inflorescence.

Perennial: A plant that lives for more than two growing seasons.

Petal: One of the segments of the corolla. White or colored.

Petiole: The stalk of a leaf.

Pinnate: A compound leaf with leaflets arranged on both sides of a midrib (as in a feather).

Pistil: The central female organ of a flower, consisting of stigma, style, and ovary.

Potentially Threatened Species: A native Ohio plant species whose natural populations are imperiled to the extent that the species could conceivably become a threatened species in the state within the foreseeable future.

Prostrate: A plant or stem lying flat on the ground.

Pubescent: Covered with short, soft hairs.

Raceme: An elongated cluster of flowers arranged singly along a central stalk, each flower with its own small stalk, as in Moth Mullein.

Ray Flowers: In the Aster Family, the outer ring of petal-like flowers that encircle the disk flowers.

Regular: Describes flowers which are symmetrical.

Rhizome: An underground stem, which produces shoots above and roots below.

Rootstock: The rhizome.

Rosette: A cluster of radiating leaves at ground level. Often the first year's growth of a biennial plant.

Sepal: One of the individual parts of the calyx, usually green, but sometimes with color.

Serrated: Toothed margin of a leaf.

Sessile: Without a stalk.

Spike: An elongated flower cluster with stalkless flowers arranged along a central stem, as in Common Mullein.

Stalk: The stem of a flower or a leaf.

Stamen: The male organ of a flower, consisting of anther and filament.

Stigma: The pollen-receiving tip of the pistil.

Stipule: A small, leaflike appendage (often in pairs), growing at the base of the petiole.

Style: The stalk of the pistil, supporting the stigma.

Threatened Species: A native Ohio plant species whose natural populations in the state are limited between four to ten occurences.

Tendril: A slender, coiling, vine-like growth structure used for climbing or support.

Umbel: A flat-topped flower cluster, somewhat resembling an umbrella, with all flower stalks radiating from the central point, as in Queen Anne's Lace.

Vein: One of a network of tiny channels in a stem and leaf through which fluids circulate throughout the plant.

Whorled: Three or more leaves or flowers arranged in a circle around a central point on a stem.

White flowers

Common Arrowhead
(Sagittaria latifolia)
Water-plantain Family (Alismataceae)

Wild Leek
(Allium tricoccum)
Lily Family (Liliaceae)

White Trout-lily
(Erythronium albidum)
Lily Family (Liliaceae)

Description White flower, 1" wide, with 3 petals, growing in a loose cluster. Distinctive leaves, arrowhead-shaped, 6–12" long. Height: 2–3 ft.

Comments Perennial. Also known as Duck Potato. This is an emergent plant growing in shallow water. The thick tubers are a favorite food of ducks, geese, and muskrats. The tubers are edible and were collected for food by early settlers and Native Americans. Native.

Range Throughout the state.

Habitat Shallow water of lakes, ponds, slow-moving streams, and swamps.

Blooming Period July–September.

Description White flowers growing in an umbel, 2" wide, at the top of a tall, leafless flower stalk. Flowers appear after the leaves have withered. Leaves large, 5–10" long, elliptical, with parallel veins and smooth margins. Height: 6–14".

Comments Perennial. Also known as Ramps. The species name comes from Greek (*tri* and *kokkos*) meaning "3-seeds" in reference to the fruit, which is a capsule that opens and exposes black seeds in groups of 3's. The juice from the plant has a strong onion odor. The bulbs are edible and are commonly used for seasoning. Native Americans and early settlers treated insect stings by rubbing the juice from a crushed bulb on the affected area of the skin. Native.

Range Throughout the state.

Habitat Rich, moist woodlands and bottomlands.

Blooming Period June–July.

Description Solitary, nodding white flower, 1–1½" long, with 3 petals and 3 petal-like sepals. Petals often tinged with lavender outside. Only 2 basal leaves, which are mottled. Height: 6–9".

Comments Perennial. Also known as White Fawn-lily. The two common names refer to the mottled leaves resembling a brook trout or a fawn. The leaves and flower stalk grow from small bulbs deep in the soil. The plants commonly propagate by offshoots from the bulbs. Because 7 years or longer are required for the production of flowers, one often finds large flowerless colonies of leaves, each leaf from a separate bulb. Native.

Range Scattered throughout the state.

Habitat Moist woodlands and thickets.

Blooming Period April–June.

Star-of-Bethlehem
(Ornithogalum umbellatum)
Lily Family (Liliaceae)

Solomon's Plume
(Smilacina racemosa)
Lily Family (Liliaceae)

Snow Trillium
(Trillium nivale)
Lily Family (Liliaceae)

Bill Denlinger

Description White flowers, 1¼" wide, with 6 petals, growing in a cluster. Green stripe on underside of each petal. Leaves grass-like, with white stripe along the midrib. Height: 4–12".

Comments Perennial. The leaves appear much earlier than the flowers. The leaves often cover a large area, giving the appearance of thick grass. The flowers open late in the morning, only in sunshine, and close in the evening. It has escaped from cultivation. Introduced from Europe and especially the Middle East.

Range Abundant in nearly one-third of Ohio counties.

Habitat Well-drained soil, rich with organic material. Fields, meadows, open woodlands, and roadsides.

Blooming Period April–June.

Description Creamy-white flowers growing in a many-flowered terminal cluster, 1–4" long. Leaves alternate. Berries red with purple spots. Stem arching and zig-zagging. Height: 1–3 ft.

Comments Perennial. The appearance of leaves is similar to those of Solomon's Seal (*Polygonatum biflorum*), which has pairs of greenish flowers hanging beneath leaf axils along the stem. Both plants commonly grow together in large numbers in moist soil, rich with organic material. Native.

Range Common throughout the state.

Habitat Moist woods, woodland slopes, and thickets.

Blooming Period May–July.

Description A solitary white flower, 1" wide. As with all Trilliums, all parts are in 3's: 3 petals, 3 sepals, 3 leaves in a whorl. Leaves oval. Height: 2–6".

Comments Perennial. This dwarf Trillium is one of our earliest spring wildflowers, blooming even while snow remains on the ground. It is declining in abundance at a significant rate. It is a rare and potentially threatened species. An increasing number of these delicate wild-flower species are threatened with extinction as their habitat is disturbed by humans. Native.

Range Confined to areas of calcareous rock outcroppings in southern Ohio.

Habitat Rich woods, shaded ledges, and at the base of limestone cliffs.

Blooming Period March–April.

Large-flowered Trillium
(Trillium grandiflorum)
Lily Family (Liliaceae)

Drooping Trillium
(Trillium flexipes)
Lily Family (Liliaceae)

Yucca
(Yucca filamentosa)
Agave Family (Agavaceae)

Description Showy white flower, 1–3" wide. Petals turn pink with age. 3 white petals, 3 green sepals, 6 stamens, 3 stigmas, and 3 leaves. Height: 6–20".

Comments Perennial. The genus name comes from Latin (*tres*) meaning "three," a perfect designation because all parts are in threes. This is the largest and showiest of our Trilliums. A spectacular display of the flowers is produced in the well-lighted conditions of the forest floor before the leaves appear on the trees. Ohio's old-growth forests usually present the greatest display of these spring wildflowers. These woodlands must be preserved so that present and future generations of people will be able to enjoy the wildflowers as one of our most valuable natural resources. This beautiful plant is the official state wildflower of Ohio. Native.

Range Abundant and widespread throughout the state, except for the northwestern counties.

Habitat Rich woods.

Blooming Period April–May.

Description White (or maroon) flower, 1–2" wide. Petals recurved. Anthers distinctively creamy-white, longer than their filaments. Ovary white. Petals, sepals, and leaves in 3's. Flower stalk 1–2" long, drooping (or horizontal). Leaves sessile. Height: 12–15".

Comments Perennial. Also known as Bent Trillium. The color of the ovary is consistant within each species of trillium. The colors of the petals are often variable. All species of trilliums bloom in the spring. The seeds contain an oil which attracts ants that carry the seeds to their nest. There the ants consume the oil as food, but do not harm the seeds, and thus the seeds are dispersed. Native.

Range Throughout the state.

Habitat Calcareous soil. Moist woods.

Blooming Period April–May.

Description White flowers, 1½" wide, nodding, bell-shaped, in a loose cluster. Stem tall, stout, growing up from a rosette of rigid, sword-like leaves. Loose threads along the leaf margins. Height: 5–10 ft.

Comments Perennial. Also known as Spanish Bayonet. It is pollinated by the yucca moth (*Tegeticula yuccasella*), which thrusts the pollen into the pistil where it will be effective, and lays her eggs in the ovary, which will ripen as food for her young. Without pollination by the moth, the Yucca would produce no seeds. Without seeds, the moth could not reproduce. This is an excellent example of symbiosis in which two organisms, one plant and one insect, are mutually benefited. It is the state flower of New Mexico. Native to southwestern United States, and escaped from cultivation.

Range Scattered throughout the state.

Habitat Roadsides, old fields, and areas of old homesteads.

Blooming Period June–September.

Slender Ladies' Tresses
(Spiranthes lacera)
Orchid Family (Orchidaceae)

Lizard's-tail
(Saururus cernuus)
Lizard's-tail Family (Saururaceae)

Pokeweed
(Phytolacca americana)
Pokeweed Family (Phytolaccaceae)

Description Small, white flowers, ¼" long, ascending in a distinctive, spiral spike. Flowers have a green spot at the center of the lip. Leaves form a basal rosette, withering before flowers bloom. Height: 4–24".

Comments Perennial. The genus name comes from the Latin (*spir*) meaning a coil. These are petite, inconspicuous orchids that bloom in late summer. With a hand lens, one can examine the lip, which curls up at the sides, forming a tube. It has a distinctive green spot, and is fringed at the tip. Native.

Range Southern and eastern counties of the state.

Habitat Dry, open woods, woodland borders, and fields.

Blooming Period August–September.

Description Tiny white flowers growing in a dense spike, 4–6" tall. The spike has a distinctive bend at the top. Leaves heart-shaped. Height: 2–5 ft.

Comments Perennial. The spike forms the "tail" of a lizard. The genus name comes from the Greek (*sauros*) meaning "lizard." With a hand lens it can be observed that individual flowers have 6–8 white stamens, but no petals or sepals. The flowers are fragrant. Native.

Range Throughout the state.

Habitat Swamps, marshes, shallow ponds, and stream margins

Blooming Period June–August.

Description Small white flowers, ¼" wide, with 5 petal-like sepals, growing in a long cluster with red stalk. Distinctive coarse, reddish stems. Height: 4–10 ft.

Comments Perennial. The berries are dark purple, hanging in long drooping clusters. *Berries are poisonous. DO NOT EAT.* However, emerging shoots can be gathered before the pink color appears, cooked, and eaten as greens. In the 19th century pokeberry juice served as dye and as ink. Many Civil War soldiers wrote letters home using a hand-made turkey quill pen and red pokeberry ink. Native.

Range Throughout the state.

Habitat Damp thickets, clearings, and roadsides.

Blooming Period July–September.

Spring Beauty
(Claytonia virginica)
Purslane Family (Portulacaceae)

Common Chickweed
(Stellaria media)
Pink Family (Caryophyllaceae)

Star Chickweed
(Stellaria pubera)
Pink Family (Caryophyllaceae)

Description White (to pink) flowers, ½–¾" wide, with 5 petals marked with darker pink veins. 1 pair of smooth, linear leaves about halfway up the flowering stem. Height: 6–12".

Comments Perennial. Named for John Clayton (1693–1773), a physician and botanist from Virginia. The flowers open in bright sunlight, close at night and during cloudy weather. The starchy, underground tubers were eaten raw or cooked as potato substitutes by Native Americans and early colonists. It is an early spring ephemeral wildflower that grows in large patches. Native.

Range Abundant throughout the state.

Habitat Moist woods, thickets, and clearings.

Blooming Period March–May.

Description White flower, ¼" wide, with 5 deeply cleft petals, at the end of sprawling stems. Petals so deeply cleft that at first they appear to be 10. Petals shorter than sepals. Leaves opposite, oval-shaped. Lower leaves with long stalks. Stem weak, much-branched, trailing up to 16" long. Height: 3–8".

Comments Annual. The growth form is short and reclining. Chickens, quail, doves, and sparrows feed heavily on the seeds. It is eaten by humans in Europe more commonly than in America. It has a spinach-like taste. Introduced from Europe.

Range Widespread throughout the state.

Habitat Roadsides, lawns, gardens, and disturbed areas.

Blooming Period One of very few plants found in bloom in almost any month of the year.

Description White flower, ½" wide, with 5 deeply cleft petals, at the top of an erect stem. Petals so deeply cleft that at first they appear to be 10. Petals longer than sepals. Dark anthers give good contrast against the white petals. Leaves opposite, sessile, 2–3" long, and very broad. Stems upright. Height: 6–12".

Comments Perennial. Divided petals are a characteristic of the Pink Family. The seeds are eaten by many kinds of game and song birds. Native.

Range Widespread through the state.

Habitat Moist woodland and rocky areas.

Blooming Period April–June.

Mouse-ear Chickweed

(Cerastium vulgatum)
Pink Family (Caryophyllaceae)

Bladder Campion

(Silene vulgaris)
Pink Family (Caryophyllaceae)

Jeanne Willis

White Campion

(Silene latifolia)
Pink Family (Caryophyllaceae)

Description White flower, ¼" wide, with 5 deeply cleft petals. Leaves opposite, hairy, ¾" long. Stem hairy and sticky. Height: 6–18".

Comments Perennial. The common name refers to the resemblance of the fuzzy leaves to a mouse's ear. The roots grow from the joints of the stems. The plants often form dense mats in lawns and dry fields. As a weed, it cannot survive cultivation practices, therefore, it can be easily be removed from a lawn by raking it away. Introduced from Europe.

Range Naturalized throughout the state.

Habitat Fields, roadsides, and disturbed areas.

Blooming Period May–September.

Description White flower, ¾" wide, with 5 deeply cleft petals. Styles 3, protruding beyond the petals. The distinctive calyx is swollen and balloon-shaped. Leaves opposite, sometimes clasping the stem. Stem smooth. Height: 8–18".

Comments Perennial. The common name refers to the heavily veined, balloon-like sac formed by the calyx directly beneath the flower. A characteristic of the Pink Family is the deeply cleft petals that often appear to be double. Introduced from Europe.

Range Naturalized throughout the state.

Habitat Fields, railways, roadsides, and disturbed areas.

Blooming Period April–August.

Description White flower, ½" wide, with 5 deeply cleft petals. Styles 5, not protruding beyond the petals. Leaves opposite, hairy. Height: 1–3 ft.

Comments Biennial. Also known as White Cockle. The flowers open at dusk and remain open through the morning of the following day. During the evening moths pollinate the flowers. Introduced from Europe.

Range Throughout the state.

Habitat Shaded roadsides, railways, meadows, and disturbed areas.

Blooming Period June–September.

Fragrant Water-lily
(Nymphaea odorata)
Water-lily Family (Nymphaeaceae)

Tall Meadow-rue
(Thalictrum pubescens)
Buttercup Family (Ranunculaceae)

Rue Anemone
(Anemonella thalictroides)
Buttercup Family (Ranunculaceae)

Jeanne Willis

Description Showy white flower, 3–5" wide, very fragrant. Stamens yellow. Blooms only from early morning until noon. Leaves round, 6–12" wide, with a single cleft.

Comments Floating on the surface, the leaves are traditionally called "lily pads." The stomata, tiny openings on the surface of leaves for exchange of carbon dioxide and oxygen, are located on the upper surface of the leaves. The flowers appear to be supported by the lily pads; however, they have separate stems. The large stems (rhizomes) buried in the mud are a favorite food of muskrats. This is our most common white Water-lily. Native.

Range Scattered throughout the state.

Habitat Ponds, shallow lakes, and quiet waters.

Blooming Period June–September.

Description White flowers, ⅓" wide. Numerous stamens in a starburst form without petals and sepals. Compound leaves divided and subdivided into many 3-lobed leaflets. Height: 3–8 ft.

Comments Perennial. In spite of the fact that there are no petals and the sepals drop as the flowers open, the clusters of white flowers are very showy. The flowers are wind-pollinated. Native.

Range Throughout the state.

Habitat Rich woods, wet meadows, and streambanks.

Blooming Period June–August.

Description White flowers, ¾" wide, with 5–10 petal-like sepals. Delicate plant with 2–3 flowers on slender stalks above a whorl of small leaflets in 3's with 3 blunt lobes. Delicate, slender stem. Height: 4–9".

Comments Perennial. For the Rue Anemone the rich forests and woodlands are stable habitats. Most of this plant's energy is spent in leaf, stem, and root growth. The flowers are produced yearly but tend to be small and few in number. This early-blooming spring ephemeral is similar to Isopyrum (*Isopyrum biternatum*), which has only 5 petal-like sepals. Native.

Range Throughout the state.

Habitat Rich woods.

Blooming Period March–May.

Thimbleweed

(Anemone virginiana)
Buttercup Family (Ranunculaceae)

Virgin's-bower

(Clematis virginiana)
Buttercup Family (Ranunculaceae)

David Dister

Description White flower (to greenish), 1" wide, with 5 petal-like sepals. Stamens numerous. The flower grows on a single stem; however, each plant will have several blossoms. Leaves stalked, divided into 3 leaflets. Stem has 3 leaves. Height: 2–3 ft.

Comments Perennial. The fruit resembles a thimble, 1" long, green at first, turning to tan with maturity. The flowers and "thimbles," on separate stems, can be present at the same time. It is similar to Canada Anemone (*A. canadensis*), which has sessile leaves. Native.

Range Throughout the state.

Habitat Old fields and dry, open woods.

Blooming Period July–August.

Description White flowers, 1" wide, with 4 petal-like sepals, growing in loose clusters in the leaf axils. Flowers fragrant. Compound leaves have 3 sharply toothed leaflets. Stem woody. The plant is a long, intertwining vine climbing over bushes and fences. Length: 10 ft.

Comments Perennial. In the autumn the distinctive fruit is a cluster of silvery-gray plumes known as "Old Man's Beard." The plant climbs by means of the leaves coiling around other plants and fences. Native.

Range Throughout the state.

Habitat Lowland areas of moist thickets, woodland borders, streambanks, and roadsides.

Blooming Period July–September.

Isopyrum
(Isopyrum biternatum)
Buttercup Family (Ranunculaceae)

White Baneberry
(Actaea alba)
Buttercup Family (Ranunculaceae)

Mayapple
(Podophyllum peltatum)
Barberry Family (Berberidaceae)

David Dister

Jeanne Willis

Description White flowers, ½–¾" wide, with 5 petal-like sepals. Delicate plant with 2–3 flowers on slender stalks above a whorl of small leaflets in 3's and deeply lobed. Height: 4–10".

Comments Perennial. This leafy, delicate plant grows from thick, fibrous roots. The woodland herbs put most of their energy into their root system, which is an adaptation that maximizes the chance of surviving the harsh winter. It is similar to Rue Anemone (*Anemonella thalictroides*), which has 5–10 petal-like sepals. Native.

Range Throughout the state.

Habitat Usually found in calcareous soil. Rich woods and thickets.

Blooming Period April–May.

Description Tiny white flowers, ¼" wide, growing in a dense rounded cluster. Triple compound leaves with sharply toothed leaflets. The fruit is a cluster, 6" long, of distinctive white berries, each having a thick red stalk and a dark purple "eye." Height: 1–2 ft.

Comments Perennial. This plant is probably more commonly recognized by its distinctive berries than its inconspicuous flowers. Also known as Doll's Eyes, in reference to the white berries that resemble the china eyes used in early dolls. The berries are borne on the plant from July through September. The term "bane" often is used in the names of poisonous plants. *The berries are poisonous. DO NOT EAT.* Native.

Range Scattered throughout the state.

Habitat Rich, moist woods, wooded floodplains, and thickets.

Blooming Period May–June.

Description Solitary white flower, 1½–2" wide, with 6–9 petals. Stamens yellow. Flower grows in a fork below 2 large, deeply cleft umbrella-like leaves. Single-leafed plants are young and do not flower. Height: 12–18".

Comments Perennial. Also known as Mandrake. Mayapples grow in colonies that make a distinctive appearance with their "umbrellas" covering the forest floor. *The leaves, roots, and green fruit are poisonous. DO NOT EAT.* However, the lemon-colored, ripe fruit is edible, and early settlers used it to make a preserve. Native.

Range Locally abundant throughout the state.

Habitat Rich woods and openings.

Blooming Period April–June.

Twinleaf
(Jeffersonia diphylla)
Barberry Family (Berberidaceae)

Bloodroot
(Sanguinaria canadensis)
Poppy Family (Papaveraceae)

Squirrel-corn
(Dicentra canadensis)
Poppy Family (Papaveraceae)

Description Solitary white flower, 1" wide, with 8 petals, growing on a leafless stalk. Leaves are basal, long-stemmed. Each leaf is deeply divided into two wing-like segments giving the appearance of a large green butterfly. Height: 6–8".

Comments Perennial. This spring ephemeral, which only blooms for a few days, is named in honor of Thomas Jefferson, the third President of the United States. The fruit is a large dry, pear-shaped pod with a tiny, hinged capsule. It slightly resembles Bloodroot (*Sanguinaria canadensis*), which has a large, divided leaf. Only one other species occurs in the world—*J. dubia,* which is native to Eastern Asia. Native.

Range Throughout the southern half of the state.

Habitat Moist, well-drained slopes and rich woods with calcareous soil.

Blooming Period April–May.

Description Solitary white flower, 1–2" wide, with 8–12 petals. Yellow stamens. Flower grows atop a smooth stalk, rising from the center of a single, curled leaf with 5–9 deep lobes. Height: 6–10".

Comments Perennial. The genus name comes from the Latin (*sanguin*) meaning "blood." The juice throughout the plant, especially the rootstock, is bright red. This is one of the eagerly anticipated spring ephemerals. Native Americans used the juice as a dye for clothing, ceremonial paint, and insect repellent. Native.

Range Locally abundant throughout the state.

Habitat Rich woods.

Blooming Period March–May.

Description Delicate white flowers, ½–¾" long, with rounded short spurs, heart-shaped, and hanging from a slightly arched stem. Leaves pale green, finely dissected, and fern-like. Flower stem leafless. Height: 6–12".

Comments Perennial. The roots are yellow tubers that somewhat resemble kernels of corn. This, combined with the behavior of squirrels digging for food, gave rise to the common name. It is somewhat toxic to cattle. This spring wildflower is closely related to Dutchman's-breeches (*D. cucullaria*). These two species are often found growing next to each other. It is related to the cultivated bleeding heart (*D. spectabilis*). Native.

Range Throughout the state.

Habitat Rich woods with deep soil.

Blooming Period April–May.

Dutchman's-breeches
(Dicentra cucullaria)
Poppy Family (Papaveraceae)

Garlic Mustard
(Alliaria petiolata)
Mustard Family (Brassicaceae)

Cut-leaved Toothwort
(Cardamine concatenata)
Mustard Family (Brassicaceae)

Description Delicate white flowers, ½"–¾" long, hanging from a slightly arched stem, with the "breeches" having their ankles up and their waists down. Leaves pale green, finely dissected, and fern-like. Flower stem leafless. Height: 5–10".

Comments Perennial. The common name refers to the resemblance of the flower to the traditional Dutch pantaloons hanging on a clothesline. The roots are small pink or white tubers. This spring ephemeral is pollinated by bumblebees that have a proboscis long enough to reach the nectar. Also known as Little Blue Staggers, referring to the poisonous (even fatal) effects on cattle should they unfortunately graze on the leaves, which contain the toxic alkaloid cucullarine. Dutchman's-breeches is closely related to Squirrel-corn (*D. canadensis*), and is often found in the same habitat. Native.

Range Throughout the state.

Habitat In calcareous soil of rich woods and floodplains.

Blooming Period April–May.

Description White flower, ⅓" wide, with 4 petals, growing at tip of stem. Leaves triangular, sharply toothed, and smell of garlic when crushed. Height: 1–3 ft.

Comments Biennial. The leaves of the 1st year are widespread and often cover very large areas of ground. Garlic Mustard is a very invasive species which threatens plant diversity by rapidly replacing native wildflowers. It is a serious "weed" throughout Ohio's woodlands. Introduced from Europe.

Range Spreading throughout the state.

Habitat Roadsides, woods, and disturbed areas.

Blooming Period April–June.

Description White flowers, ½–1" wide, with 4 petals, in a loose terminal cluster. Petals take on a pinkish cast as they get older. Whorl of 3 leaves, each divided into 3–5 narrow, sharp-toothed leaflets. Height: 8–15".

Comments Perennial. The common name describes the deeply divided leaves and the tooth-like shape of the fleshy tubers. "Wort" is an old English word meaning "plant." As with many early-blooming spring wildflowers, Toothwort is pollinated by a variety of insect species. Native.

Range Common throughout the state.

Habitat Rich woods.

Blooming Period April–May.

Spring Cress
(Cardamine rhomboidea)
Mustard Family (Brassicaceae)

Wild Stonecrop
(Sedum ternatum)
Stonecrop Family (Crassulaceae)

Miterwort
(Mitella diphylla)
Saxifrage Family (Saxifragaceae)

Description White flower, ¾" wide, with 4 petals. Stem leaves alternate. Basal leaves form a rosette of round leaves with long petioles. Stem smooth and sturdy. Height: 8–20".

Comments Perennial. All plants of the Mustard Family have 4 petals which form a cross. The alternative family name, Cruciferae, comes from the Latin (*cruci*) meaning "cross." Spring Cress is a plant of wet areas. It is similar to Purple Cress (*C. douglassii*), which has purple petals and a hairy stem. Native.

Range Throughout the state.

Habitat Rich wet woods, wet clearings, springs, and wet streambanks.

Blooming Period April–June.

Description White flowers, ½" wide, with 4–5 petals, growing in a 3-branched terminal cluster. Anthers purple. Leaves thick, succulent, crowded at tips of non-flowering branches. Stems 6–15" long.

Comments Perennial. Stonecrops are succulent herbs with star-shaped flowers in branched clusters. They often grow in large colonies forming mats covering shaded, moist rocks in the woods. Their cultivated relatives include Jade Plant, Air Plant, Live Forever, and Hen-and-Chicks. These plants reproduce commonly by means of vegetative propagation. Native.

Range Throughout the state.

Habitat Damp rocks, banks, and moist wooded cliffs.

Blooming Period April–June.

Description Tiny, delicate, white flowers, ⅛" wide, with 5 petals, growing in a raceme. Petals have a delicate fringe so each flower resembles a snowflake. A single pair of toothed, opposite leaves midway on the stem is responsible for the species name. Basal leaves are long, oval-shaped, and lobed. Slender stem. Height: 6–18".

Comments Perennial. The cup-shaped flowers give rise to the common name "Bishop's Cap." The common name comes from the Greek (*mitra*) meaning "little cap." Close examination with a hand lens is necessary to appreciate their exquisite beauty. Native.

Range Throughout the state.

Habitat Rich woods.

Blooming Period April–May

Goatsbeard
(Aruncus dioicus)
Rose Family (Rosaceae)

Wild Strawberry
(Fragaria virginiana)
Rose Family (Rosaceae)

White Avens
(Geum canadense)
Rose Family (Rosaceae)

Description A showy, distinctive display of minute, white flowers in long, feathery, twisting spikes. Leaves pinnately compound, divided 2–3 times. Height: 3–7 ft.

Comments Perennial. The common name refers to the appearance, from a distance, of the bloom to the beard of a goat. The species name comes from the Greek (*di* and *oikos*) meaning "in two households" and refers to the male (staminate) and female (pistillate) flowers that grow on separate plants. Native.

Range Mostly in the hill country of eastern and southern Ohio.

Habitat Rich woods, ravines, and wooded roadside banks.

Blooming Period May–July.

Description White flower, ½"–1" wide, usually shorter than the leaves. Flowers sometimes in clusters. Stamens numerous. Recognized by the leaves, which are divided into 3 sharp-toothed leaflets on long stalks. Height: 3–6".

Comments Perennial. The plant propagates by means of runners. The plant with its long runners acts as a soil anchor to prevent erosion. The fruit is red, juicy, and edible by birds and mammals, as well as humans. Cultivated strawberries (*F. ananassa*) are hybrids from this species. Native.

Range Throughout the state.

Habitat Open fields and meadows.

Blooming Period April–June.

Description White flower, ½" wide, with 5 petals. Leaves divided into 3's. Stem smooth. Height: 18–30".

Comments Perennial. With a hand lens, look for a crook in the long slender style just beneath the stigma. The fruits have hooks which are easily caught in animal fur, aiding in their dispersal. Native.

Range Throughout the state.

Habitat Shaded places, woods edges, and thickets.

Blooming Period June–August.

Blackberry
(Rubus allegheniensis)
Rose Family (Rosaceae)

Canadian Burnet
(Sanguisorba canadensis)
Rose Family (Rosaceae)

White Clover
(Trifolium repens)
Pea Family (Fabaceae)

Description White flowers, 1" wide, with 5 petals, growing in racemes. Flower stalks hairy. Leaflets 3. Stems erect to arching, with numerous prickles. Stems reddish and often grooved. Height: 2–8 ft.

Comments As the fruit matures the berries progress through a series of color changes from green, to red, to black. The juicy, black berries are a favorite for making pies and jellies. They are also an important food source for wildlife. Native.

Range Common throughout the state.
Habitat Roadsides and fields.
Blooming Period May–July.

Description Small white flowers growing in a spike, 2–5" tall. Leaves pinnately compound, with 7–15 toothed leaflets. Height: 1–6 ft.

Comments Perennial. Examination of the flowers with a hand lens reveals that they have 4 petal-like sepals and long stamens which account for their fuzzy appearance. The genus name comes from the Latin (*sanguin* and *sorbere*) meaning "blood" and "to swallow." It is reported that ancient people believed plants of this genus could be used to stop bleeding. Native.

Range Scattered throughout the state.
Habitat Swamps, bogs, wet meadows, and wet prairies.
Blooming Period July–October.

Description White (or tinged with pink), round flower head, ½" wide. Flowers and leaves growing on separate stalks from creeping runners. Leaflets 3, in familiar "clover-leaf." Pale "V" (chevron) on each leaflet. Height: 4–10".

Comments Perennial. White Clover is pollinated by honeybees. As with other members of Fabaceae, this plant is capable of capturing gaseous nitrogen from the atmosphere and converting it into a usable form through a process called nitrogen-fixation. This is accomplished by bacteria living within nodules in the roots. Thus, clover is often planted as a cover crop which will enrich the soil with nitrogen. It is also a very important forage crop for agriculture. Introduced from Europe.

Range Throughout the state.
Habitat Field edges, roadsides, and lawns.
Blooming Period May–October.

White Sweet Clover
(Melilotus alba)
Pea Family (Fabaceae)

Striped White Violet
(Viola striata)
Violet Family (Violaceae)

Biennial Gaura
(Gaura biennis)
Evening-primrose Family (Onagraceae)

Description White flowers in spike, 2–4" long. Leaves with 3 leaflets. Leaves give sweet odor when crushed. Height: 3–8 ft.

Comments Biennial. As with other members of Fabaceae, White Sweet Clover is widely used as a pasture crop for nitrogen enrichment of the soil. People marvel at the honeybee tirelessly buzzing from flower to flower, taking from each a drop of nectar which eventually will be converted into honey in the hive. But equally important for the flowers is the role of the honeybee as the most reliable and active agent for transfer of pollen from the anther to the stigma. This plant is similar to Yellow Sweet Clover (*M. officinalis*), which has yellow flowers. Introduced from Europe.

Range Abundant throughout the state.
Habitat Roadsides and field edges.
Blooming Period May–October.

Description White flower, ½" wide, with prominent dark veins at base of petals. Leaves and flowers on the same stalk. Stem green, smooth, with long, toothed stipules. Height: 6–12".

Comments Perennial. Violets have a distinctive arrangement of 5 petals, with the lower petal veined and spurred at the base. The common White Violet is similar to the Canadian Violet (*V. canadensis*), which has a purple, hairy stem with small stipules. Native.

Range Throughout the state.
Habitat Low, moist woodlands, streambanks, wet fields, and roadsides.
Blooming Period April–June.

Description White flowers (turning pink with age), ½" wide, with 4 petals. Stamens 8, long and conspicuous, drooping beneath the flower. Stigma cross-shaped. Flowers bloom 2 or 3 at a time on slender spikes. Sepals reflexed. Leaves lance-shaped, slightly toothed. Height: 2–5 ft.

Comments Biennial. Due to its size this petite summer wildflower is easily overlooked. Its beauty can be better appreciated by examination with a hand lens. Native.

Range Throughout the state.
Habitat Fields and meadows.
Blooming Period June–October.

Sweet Cicely
(Osmorhiza longistylis)
Parsley Family (Apiaceae)

Harbinger-of-spring
(Erigenia bulbosa)
Parsley Family (Apiaceae)

Poison Hemlock
(Conium maculatum)
Parsley Family (Apiaceae)

Description. Tiny white flowers growing in umbels at the tops of the stems. Fern-like leaves are 3 times compoundly divided. Height: 1–3 ft.

Comments Perennial. When crushed, the leaves, stems, and roots have the distinctive odor of licorice or anise. Early settlers used the root for flavoring in cookies and candies. The seeds are barbed and easily stick to animal fur which aids in their dispersal. It is similar to *O. claytonii,* which lacks the odor of anise. Native.

Range Throughout the state.

Habitat Moist but well-drained soil in shady woods.

Blooming Period May–June.

Description Tiny white flowers, ¼" wide, with 5 petals, growing in small umbels. Leaves (1 or 2) on the stem, divided into narrow or oblong segments, often not fully developed at flowering time. Height: 4–9".

Comments Perennial. Also known as Pepper-and-salt because of the contrast of the dark stamens against the white petals. This is one of Ohio's earliest spring wildflowers. Native.

Range Throughout most of the state.

Habitat Wooded floodplains, open woods, terraces, and slopes.

Blooming Period March–April.

Description Tiny white flowers growing in umbels, 2–4" wide. A large, much-branched plant. Leaves finely divided and fernlike. Base of leaves enlarged and sheathing the stem. Stem spotted with purple. Height: 2–10 ft.

Comments Biennial. The plant was used to poison the Greek philosopher Socrates (470–399 B.C.). *Deadly poisonous. DO NOT EAT.* It also can be toxic to cattle. Introduced from Europe.

Range Throughout much of the state, especially central, south-central, and southwestern counties.

Habitat Roadsides, railways, riverbanks, and other disturbed weedy areas.

Blooming Period May–August.

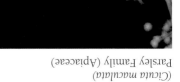

David Dister

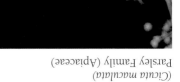

Water Hemlock
(*Cicuta maculata*)
Parsley Family (Apiaceae)

Queen Anne's Lace
(*Daucus carota*)
Parsley Family (Apiaceae)

Spotted Wintergreen
(*Chimaphila maculata*)
Pyrola Family (Pyrolaceae)

Description White flowers, growing in umbels, 2–4" wide. Leaves 2–3 times compound. Leaflets lance-shaped, toothed. Stem much-branched, spotted with purple, especially at the joints. Height: 3–6 ft.

Comments Perennial. Also known as Spotted Cowbane because cattle have died from grazing on it. *Deadly poisonous. DO NOT EAT.* It is similar to Poison Hemlock (*Conium maculatum*), which has fern-like leaves. Native.

Range Throughout the state.

Habitat Margins of ponds and lakes, streambanks, swamps, and wet ditches.

Blooming Period June–July.

Description White flowers in an umbel, 2–4" wide. Often 1 deep purple floret in the center. Leaves finely divided and subdivided. Stem bristly. Height: 1–3 ft.

Comments Biennial. Also known as Wild Carrot. The garden carrot is the same species. When garden carrots are allowed to go to seed, the similarity between the flowers becomes apparent. The long taproot forms the first year and is edible, either raw or cooked. Often, entire fields are whitened by the lacy, flat flower-tops of Queen Anne's Lace. After their bloom, the old umbels curl to form a cuplike "bird's nest." It is reported that Queen Anne of England decorated her hair with these attractive white flowers. Introduced from Europe.

Range Throughout the state.

Habitat Roadsides, railways, open dry fields, and other disturbed areas.

Blooming Period June–November.

Description White (or pink) flowers, ¾" wide, with 5 petals, nodding, growing in a small cluster. Flowers fragrant, waxy. Leaves whorled, white stripe along the midrib. Stem erect. Height: 4–10".

Comments Perennial. Although the common name is "spotted," the dark green leaves actually are white "striped." The distinctive leaves are green throughout the year. These evergreen leaves are a good contrast against the brown litter of the forest floor. The fruit is a brown capsule which persists through the winter. Native.

Range Mostly in the eastern half of the state.

Habitat Acid soil, sandy soil, dry woods, especially under conifers and oaks.

Blooming Period June–August.

Indian Pipe
(Monotropa uniflora)
Indian Pipe Family (Monotropaceae)

Shooting Star
(Dodecatheon meadia)
Primrose Family (Primulaceae)

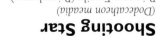

Enchanter's Nightshade
(Circaea lutetiana)
Evening-primrose Family (Onagraceae)

Description Solitary, nodding, white flower, 1" long, with 4–5 petals, atop a white stem. Leaves lack color, are scale-like on the stem. Height: 4–10".

Comments Perennial. At first the flower is nodding, forming the "pipe." Later it becomes erect when the fruit is formed. Also known as Corpse Plant. The plant turns black when the fruit ripens. Since the plant lacks chlorophyll and lives on dead organic matter, it is a saprophyte. The roots are surrounded by fungi (mycorrhiza) so that the roots themselves do not come into contact with the soil but receive their nourishment from the fungi, which in turn obtain their nutrients from decaying woody plant material. Indian Pipe cannot live without the assistance of the fungi. Native.

Range Found in eastern Ohio and at scattered sites in the western counties.

Habitat Rich woodlands.

Blooming Period June–August.

Description White (pink or lavender) flower, with 5 petals, reflexed and pointing upward, forming a star-like shape. Stamens form a pointed beak downward. Leaves basal only, forming a rosette. Stem without leaves. Height: 1–2 ft.

Comments Perennial. Also known as Pride of Ohio. There are no known uses, but its striking beauty makes it a unique wildflower. In earlier times, Shooting Star was plentiful. Excessive picking and destruction of its habitat have significantly reduced its population. Native.

Range Southwestern quarter of the state, with some at scattered sites in the northeastern counties.

Habitat Prairie openings, woodland openings, and dolomite cliffs.

Blooming Period April–June.

Description Small white flowers, ¼" wide, with 2 deeply divided petals, growing in loose terminal clusters. Leaves opposite, toothed. Height: 1–2 ft.

Comments Perennial. The genus is named after Circe, the enchantress from Greek mythology, who gave potions made from this plant to the companions of Odysseus and turned them into swine. Close examination reveals the petals are so deeply notched that they appear as 4 petals. The fruit is a small bur bearing numerous hooked bristles. These easily attach to animal fur and thus are widely dispersed. Native.

Range Throughout the state.

Habitat Rich woods and wooded floodplains.

Blooming Period June–August.

Wild Potato-vine
(Ipomoea pandurata)
Morning-glory Family (Convolvulaceae)

Whorled Milkweed
(Asclepias verticillata)
Milkweed Family (Asclepiadaceae)

Indian Hemp
(Apocynum cannabinum)
Dogbane Family (Apocynaceae)

Description Small white (or greenish) flowers, ¼" long, in erect clusters. Corolla pointing upward. Leaves smooth, opposite, and oblong. One erect main stem (reddish-purple) with sterile side branches. Height: 1–4 ft.

Comments Perennial. The members of this family are called Dogbane, because early Native Americans mixed a potion of this common plant as a remedy (unsuccessful) against all poisons, parasitic worms, and mad-dog disease (rabies). Broken stems and leaves release a milky juice. Seed pods 6–8" long. Seeds are borne on feathery tufts and are dispersed by wind. The common name, Indian Hemp, reflects its tough, fibrous bark, which was used for cordage by Native Americans and early settlers. It is similar to Spreading Dogbane (*A. androsaemifolium*), which has pink flowers. Native.

Range Throughout the state.

Habitat Moist fields and thickets, pond and stream margins, moist woodland borders.

Blooming Period June–September.

Description White (to greenish) flowers, ¼" long, growing in clusters, often in leaf axils. Flowers fragrant. Leaves very narrow, in whorls of 3–6. Height: 1–2 ft.

Comments Perennial. The extremely narrow, whorled leaves may cause one to mistake this plant for something other than a milkweed. However, close examination of the flowers with their distinctive corolla lobes and hoods discloses their identity. Native.

Range At scattered sites in the western half of the state.

Habitat Dry fields, open woods, and roadsides.

Blooming Period June–September.

Description Funnel-shaped white flowers, 2–3" long, with deep purple throats. Leaves heart-shaped. A trailing vine up to 15 feet long.

Comments Perennial. Also known as Man-of-the-Earth. The Wild Potato-vine commonly climbs fences and low shrubs. It has a very large tuberous root which, when roasted, is edible. The root grows to be several feet long with reports given of weights of about 20 pounds. Native.

Range Southern Ohio counties and at scattered sites northward.

Habitat Dry soil, hillsides, roadsides, and fields.

Blooming Period July–September.

Large-leaved Waterleaf
(*Hydrophyllum macrophyllum*)
Waterleaf Family (Hydrophyllaceae)

Hedge Bindweed
(*Calystegia sepium*)
Morning-glory Family (Convolvulaceae)

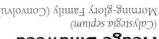

Field Bindweed
(*Convolvulus arvensis*)
Morning-glory Family (Convolvulaceae)

Description White (to pink) funnel-shaped flowers, ¾" long. Resembles a morning glory, but smaller. Leaves arrow-shaped. Slender, trailing stem.

Comments Perennial. Field Bindweed is a troublesome weed in cultivated fields and gardens. It is similar to Hedge Bindweed (*Calystegia sepium*), which has larger flowers and leaves. Introduced from Europe.

Range Naturalized throughout much of the state.

Habitat Roadsides, railways, and disturbed areas.

Blooming Period June–September.

Description Showy white (or pink) funnel-shaped flowers, 2" long. 2 distinctive, large bracts surrounding the calyx. Flower open during the morning hours, closed in afternoon. Leaves arrowhead-shaped. Stems twining and climbing from 3–10 ft. long.

Comments Perennial. A vine is a growth form, not a classification of plants. The vines grow densely, climbing other plants and fences. Like several other common members of the Morning-glory Family, Hedge Bindweed occurs frequently in the early stages of old field succession. In some places it becomes an undesirable weed, difficult to eradicate without removing all of the roots. Native.

Range Throughout the state.

Habitat Riverbanks, beaches, fields, fencerows, roadsides, railways, and other disturbed areas.

Blooming Period June–October.

Description Pale violet (to white) flowers, ½" long, growing in clusters at the tips of long stalks. Stamens protruding beyond petals. Distinctive leaves with 5–7 lobes, mottled as though water-stained. Stem hairy. Height: 1–3 ft.

Comments Perennial. The genus name is derived from the Greek (*hydros* and *phyllon*) meaning "water-leaf" in reference to the appearance of the white spots on the leaves. Close examination reveals that the individual flowers are actually bell-shaped with protruding stamens. This wildflower can be easily identified early in the spring before the flowers bloom by the appearance of the large, distinctive leaves on the forest floor. It is similar to Virginia Waterleaf (*H. virginianum*), which has a smooth stem. Native.

Range Throughout the state.

Habitat Rich woods, thickets, and wooded floodplains.

Blooming Period May–June.

Catnip
(Nepeta cataria)
Mint Family (Lamiaceae)

Narrow-leaved Mountain-mint
(Pycnanthemum tenuifolium)
Mint Family (Lamiaceae)

Horse-nettle
(Solanum carolinense)
Nightshade Family (Solanaceae)

Description White flowers, ½" long, growing in dense terminal and axillary clusters. Petals with purple dots. Leaves opposite, toothed. When crushed, leaves give mint scent. Stems square, covered with soft, white, downy hairs. Height: 1–3 ft.

Comments Perennial. *Nepeta* is the Latin genus name for several of the mints. The species *cataria* is from the Latin meaning "associated with a cat." Catnip attracts cats, which enjoy rolling in the living plant or playing with a small toy mouse stuffed with the dried leaves. The plant contains the chemical nepeta lactone, which is a natural insect repellent. It was formerly cultivated and later escaped. Introduced from Europe.

Range Naturalized throughout the state.

Habitat Roadsides, pastures, and disturbed areas.

Blooming Period June–September.

Description Tiny white flowers in numerous, dense clusters. Leaves very narrow. Stem square, branched. Height: 1–3 ft.

Comments Perennial. In spite of the common name, these plants are found far from the mountains. However, they are found primarily in the hill country of Ohio. When crushed, the leaves and stem give off a faint mint odor. Native.

Range Eastern and southern part of the state.

Habitat Dry fields, woodland openings, and roadside banks.

Blooming Period July–September.

Description White (to pale blue) flower, 1" wide, with 5 petals. Bright yellow stamens form a central cone. Stems and leaves covered with numerous yellow prickles. Leaves alternate, toothed, and slightly lobed. Height: 1–4 ft.

Comments Perennial. It is in the same family as the potato, tomato, and tobacco. Many birds eat the yellow berries and thus disperse the seeds. Considered to be a weed by some, it is difficult to eradicate because of the deep rhizomes. Gloves should be worn while handling this plant. Native.

Range Throughout the state.

Habitat Streambanks, roadsides, railways, cultivated fields, barnyards, and other disturbed areas.

Blooming Period May–September.

Moth Mullein
(Verbascum blattaria)
Snapdragon Family (Scrophulariaceae)

Turtlehead
(Chelone glabra)
Snapdragon Family (Scrophulariaceae)

Foxglove Beardtongue
(Penstemon digitalis)
Snapdragon Family (Scrophulariaceae)

Cindy Tucci

Description White (or yellow) flower, 1" wide, with 5 petals, tinged with purple at the base, growing in a raceme. Stamens with purple hairs. Leaves alternate, toothed. Stem hairy. Height: 2–4 ft.

Comments Biennial. The white-flowered forms are more frequent than the yellow-... ...e common name refers to ... which resemble the anten-... riments have demonstrated ... viable for more than 100 ... rom Europe. ...ed throughout the state.

Habitat Dry sandy-gravelly soils of fields, roadsides, railways, and disturbed areas.

Blooming Period May–October.

Description White (tinged with pink) flower, 1" long, growing in a cluster at the tip of the stem. The upper lip arches over the lower lip. Leaves opposite, toothed. Height: 1–3 ft.

Comments Perennial. The genus name comes from the Greek (*chelone*) meaning "tortoise." The common name refers to the similarity in appearance to the head of a turtle with an open mouth. The lower lip serves as a "landing pad" for bees in search of nectar. The bees force their way deep into the throat of the flower, carrying pollen from one flower to another. Early settlers and Native Americans prepared a tonic and laxative from the leaves. Native.

Range Throughout the state.

Habitat Stream and lake borders, swamps, roadside ditches, and other wet areas.

Blooming Period July–September.

Description White (to pale pink) flowers, 1" long, with 5 petals, forming a tube, growing in clusters at top of stalk. Leaves opposite. Stem smooth. Height: 2–4 ft.

Comments Perennial. Also known as White Beardtongue. One of the 5 stamens is sterile and does not produce pollen. It is often modified into a hairy or "bearded tongue" and is an adaptation to attract insects for pollination. Native.

Range Grows throughout most of the the state, but absent from west-central and north-western counties. Sometimes locally abundant.

Habitat Old fields, roadsides, railways, and woodland openings.

Blooming Period May–July.

Culver's-root
(Veronicastrum virginicum)
Snapdragon Family (Scrophulariaceae)

English Plantain
(Plantago lanceolata)
Plantain Family (Plantaginaceae)

Partridge-berry
(Mitchella repens)
Madder Family (Rubiaceae)

Description Small white flowers growing in spikes, 2–6" tall. Leaves lance-shaped, toothed, in whorls of 3–7. Stem smooth. Height: 2–7 ft.

Comments Perennial. Examination with a hand lens of the individual flowers reveals they are tubular, with 2 projecting stamens. There are only 2 species in this genus. The other one is in Asia. Native.

Range More common in the eastern half, less common in the western half of the state.

Habitat Woods, thickets, moist meadows, roadsides, and railways.

Blooming Period July–October.

Description Tiny white flowers in a short, dense spike. Leaves long and narrow with 3 ribs. Stalk long and grooved. Height: 9–24".

Comments Perennial. Also known as Buckhorn Plantain. The leaves are a favorite food of rabbits. It is often a troublesome weed in lawns and gardens. Introduced from Europe.

Range Naturalized throughout most of the state.

Habitat Roads, railways, lawns, fields, and disturbed areas.

Blooming Period May–August.

Description White (to pink) flowers, ½" long, growing in pairs at the ends of the branches. Individual flower funnel-shaped, flaring into 4 lobes. Leaves opposite, round, white-veined, and green throughout the year. Length: 4–12".

Comments Perennial. The genus is named for John Mitchell (1676–1768), a botanist from Virginia. He corresponded frequently with Carolus Linnaeus (1707–1778), the Swedish botanist who developed the binomial system of taxonomy. The stem creeps along the surface of the ground, branching freely and rooting at the joints. There are only 2 species worldwide in the genus; the other one is in Japan. The fruit is a red berry which is edible by wildlife and humans. Native.

Range Mostly in the eastern and southern counties of the state.

Habitat In acid soil of woodlands.

Blooming Period June–July.

Buttonbush
(Cephalanthus occidentalis)
Madder Family (Rubiaceae)

Japanese Honeysuckle
(Lonicera japonica)
Honeysuckle Family (Caprifoliaceae)

Amur Honeysuckle
(Lonicera maackii)
Honeysuckle Family (Caprifoliaceae)

Description Spherical white flower heads, 1" wide. Leaves opposite (or in whorls of 3's), oval with pointed ends, margin entire. A shrub or small tree. Height: 3–10 ft.

Comments With a hand lens it can be observed that the flower head is composed of 100–200 tubular flowers with protruding styles. It is pollinated by a variety of insects. Buttonbush is a common pioneer plant growing on river bars. It is intolerant of shade, and often forms very dense thickets which are difficult to penetrate. Native.

Range Throughout the state.

Habitat Edges of ponds and lakes, marshes, floodplains, and streamsides.

Blooming Period June–August.

Description White flowers (yellow with age), 1 to 1½" long. Petals form a tube, with stamens projecting beyond the petals. Very fragrant. Leaves opposite. Berries black. Plant is a vine covering the ground and bushes.

Comments This plant has been known to grow as much as 30 ft. in a single year and is very difficult to eradicate. It forms dense tangles, engulfing woodland edges, and shades out young trees. It is an abundant source of food and cover for wildlife, but unfortunately it crowds out equally and more desirable species and has become a serious threat to plant diversity. Once widely cultivated, then escaped. Introduced from Asia.

Range Naturalized in all except some northwestern and west-central counties. Abundant in parts of southern Ohio.

Habitat Roadsides, thickets, woods edges, and disturbed woodlands.

Blooming Period May–July.

Description White flower (sometimes tinged with pink) changing to yellowish. Lip and tube about equal length, 1" long. Flowers in pairs in upper axils of leaves all along the stem. Berries red. Leaves opposite, long-pointed. Stem hollow. Upright shrub 10–15 ft. tall.

Comments Also known as Bush Honeysuckle. The plant is named for Richard Maack, the Russian plant explorer who collected specimens in 1855 near the Amur River in eastern China. It has escaped from botanical gardens and presently is one of the greatest threats to woodland plant diversity, as the species can form nearly pure monocultures in woodland understories. Introduced from Asia.

Range Naturalized in southern counties of the state and at scattered sites northward.

Habitat Thickets, disturbed woods, old fields, and roadsides.

Blooming Period May–June.

Elderberry
(Sambucus canadensis)
Honeysuckle Family (Caprifoliaceae)

Boneset
(Eupatorium perfoliatum)
Aster Family (Asteraceae)

Tall Thoroughwort
(Eupatorium altissimum)
Aster Family (Asteraceae)

Praire

Description White flowers growing in an umbel, 3–6" wide. Fragrant. Leaflets 7 (may be 5–11), sharply toothed. Berries dark purple to black. Stems woody but soft, with large white pith. Plant is a shrub, 4–10 ft. tall.

Comments The genus name comes from the Greek (*sambuce*) an ancient musical instrument, and refers to the soft pith, easily removed from the twigs and used to make flutes and whistles. The tangy fruits have been collected in late summer and autumn for pies, jelly, and wine. The fruits are eagerly consumed by birds in late summer. Native.

Range Throughout the state.

Habitat Wet ground at margins of swamps, marshes, ponds and streams, fencerows, and woodland borders.

Blooming Period June–July.

Description Small white flowers growing in an umbel, 4–6" wide. Leaves opposite, joined at the stem. Stem hairy, branched at the top. Height: 2–5 ft.

Comments Perennial. The species name comes from the Latin (*per* and *folia*) meaning "through the leaves" in reference to the stem appearing to penetrate the joined leaves. The leaves contain eupatorin, a glucoside once used medicinally as a tonic and an emetic. Early Native Americans used preparations of Boneset to treat fevers, colds, and battle wounds. Native.

Range Throughout the state.

Habitat Wet low ground, streambanks, swamps, other wet areas.

Blooming Period July–October.

Description White flowers growing in an umbel. Leaves opposite, lance-shaped, tapering at both ends, 3 distinctive veins, slightly toothed. Stem hairy. Height: 2–6 ft.

Comments Perennial. Also known as Tall Boneset. These plants occur abundantly in certain areas in the late summer. Examination with a hand lens reveals that they have only tube-type disk flowers without any ray flowers present. In addition the umbel is divided into smaller flower heads each consisting of only 5 flowers. Native.

Range Scattered throughout the state.

Habitat Woodland clearings and borders, fields, railways, and roadsides.

Blooming Period August–September.

White Snakeroot
(Eupatorium rugosum)
Aster Family (Asteraceae)

Calico Aster
(Aster lateriflorus)
Aster Family (Asteraceae)

Heath Aster
(Aster pilosus)
Aster Family (Asteraceae)

Description Fuzzy white flower head growing in an umbel. Leaves opposite, stemmed, sharply toothed, and usually with 3 main veins. Stem smooth. Height: 1–5 ft.

Comments Perennial. Pioneer families would often permit their family milk cows to graze in the woodlands before they had been cleared for pastures. Cattle that fed on White Snakeroot would incorporate toxins from the plant into their milk. Anyone who consumed the tainted milk would be poisoned. This "Milk Sickness" is reported to have caused the death of Abraham Lincoln's mother, Nancy Hanks Lincoln, on October 5, 1818. Native.

Range Common throughout the state.

Habitat Rich woods and thickets.

Blooming Period July–October.

Description Small white (turning reddish-purple with age) flower heads, ½" wide, with 9–15 rays. Disk purple. Leaves lance-shaped, rough, and toothed. Height: 1–4 ft.

Comments Perennial. These delicate flower heads grow on the many branches at the top of the plant. Look for flowers with various colors on the same plant at the same time. With a hand lens, look for the distinctive green midrib on the bracts of the involucre. Native.

Range Common throughout most of the state, except for some northwestern counties.

Habitat Fields, open woodlands, and thickets.

Blooming Period August–October.

Description Numerous white flower heads, ½" wide, with 15–30 rays. Disk yellow. Leaves lance-shaped and small between the flower heads. Stem hairy, much-branched. Height: 1–5 ft.

Comments Perennial. These erect, bushy asters are very common in Ohio. Many people regard asters as weeds, but their bright flowers add significantly to the beautiful colors of the autumn landscape. The seeds are an important food for songbirds throughout the fall and winter. Native.

Range Throughout the state.

Habitat Open, dry, old fields, roadsides, and disturbed areas.

Blooming Period August–October.

White-top
(Erigeron strigosus)
Aster Family (Asteraceae)

Daisy Fleabane
(Erigeron annuus)
Aster Family (Asteraceae)

Philadelphia Fleabane
(Erigeron philadelphicus)
Aster Family (Asteraceae)

Description White (to pink) flower head, ½–1" wide, with 100 or more ray flowers. Disk yellow. Several flower heads, each at the end of a branch. Distinctive leaves clasp the stem. Stem slightly hairy. Height: 6–30".

Comments Biennial. Also known as Common Fleabane. This is the earliest Fleabane to bloom. In early times, Fleabane was used to rid places of fleas. The crushed plant produced juices which were applied as a lotion to the body. The dried plant was burned as a fumigant. Native.

Range Common throughout the state.

Habitat Fields, roadsides, and open woods.

Blooming Period April–August.

Description Numerous white flower heads, ½" wide, with 40–70 ray flowers. Disk yellow. Distinctive leaves that do not clasp the stem. Leaves hairy and toothed. Stem covered with spreading hairs. Height: 1–5 ft.

Comments Annual. Resembling a small aster, this plant with its many flower heads spends large amounts of energy on reproduction to assure its survival in disturbed areas. It is similar to White-top (*E. strigosus*), which has leaves with smooth margins. Native.

Range Throughout the state.

Habitat Fields, roadsides, and disturbed areas.

Blooming Period June–October.

Description Numerous white flower heads, ½" wide, with 50–100 ray flowers. Disk yellow. Distinctive narrow, lance-shaped leaves with smooth margin. Stem covered with hairs that are lying flat against the stem. Height: 1–3 ft.

Comments Annual. It is similar to Daisy Fleabane (*E. annuus*), which has wider, toothed leaves. Native.

Range Common throughout the state.

Habitat Fields, roadsides, and disturbed areas.

Blooming Period May–September.

Yarrow
(*Achillea millefolium*)
Aster Family (Asteraceae)

Small-flowered Leafcup
(*Polymnia canadensis*)
Aster Family (Asteraceae)

Pussytoes
(*Antennaria neglecta*)
Aster Family (Asteraceae)

Description Tiny white flower heads, ¼", in a cluster at top of stem, resembling a cat's paw. Leaves in a basal rosette; each having 1 main vein. Stem woolly. Height: 4–12".

Comments Perennial. The seeds are too tiny to be significant as wildlife food, but several kinds of mammals relish the tender rosettes of leaves. The plant grows in poor, dry soils where few others will survive. It is effective in preventing soil erosion. Native.

Range Common at scattered sites throughout the state.

Habitat Well-drained soils, dry fields, and pastures.

Blooming Period April–May.

Description Tiny white flowers, with 5 ray flowers, growing in terminal clusters. Leaves distinctive, large, with 3–5 deeply cut lobes. Stem rough and hairy. Height: 2–5 ft.

Comments Perennial. The large, coarse leaves are quite visible from early on in the spring. Most of the energy spent by this woodland plant goes toward vegetative growth. In the very small flower heads only the outer flowers are fertile and will develop seeds. Native.

Range Common in moist woodlands throughout the state.

Habitat Usually found in calcareous soil. Moist, shaded, rich woods.

Blooming Period June–October.

Description White flowers growing in an umbel, 2–4" wide. Individual flowers have 4–6 rays that are 3-toothed. Distinctive leaves alternate, soft, fern-like, and aromatic when crushed. Height: 1–3 ft.

Comments Perennial. Named for the Greek hero Achilles, who is reported to have used Yarrow to stop the bleeding of his soldiers' wounds. The species name comes from the Latin (*mille* and *folia*) meaning "thousand leaves," referring to the numerous leaflets of the finely divided leaves. Yarrow grows where habitat change is rapid. The large amount of energy that is spent on reproduction is an adaptation for its survival. This is evident by the presence of large numbers of flowers in proportion to the small leaves. Native Americans and early settlers used Yarrow tea for treatment of colds and fever. Introduced from Europe.

Range Common throughout the state.

Habitat Roadsides, railways, open fields, and disturbed areas.

Blooming Period June–October.

Ox-eye Daisy
(Chrysanthemum leucanthemum)
Aster Family (Asteraceae)

Stinking Chamomile
(Anthemis cotula)
Aster Family (Asteraceae)

Description White flowers, 1" wide, with 10–20 ray flowers, yellow disk flowers. Leaves finely divided. When crushed, leaves emit a distinctive strong, disagreeable odor. Height: 8–20".

Comments Annual. Also known as Dog Fennel. The plant is common and often abundant, producing masses of white flowers. The yellow disk flowers persist long after the ray flowers have withered and dropped. This weed is capable of producing a burning sensation on wet skin. If eaten by cattle, the milk can have an unpleasant taste. Introduced from Europe.

Range Throughout the state.

Habitat Roadsides, fallow fields, barnyards, and disturbed areas.

Blooming Period May–October.

Description Solitary white daisy, 1–2" wide, with 15–20 white rays. Disk yellow, depressed in center. Leaves dark green, alternate, and bluntly toothed or lobed. Stem solitary, smooth. Height: 1–3 ft.

Comments Perennial. Also known as Marguerite Daisy. In the drama *Faust,* by Johann Goethe (1749–1832), Marguerite sang the refrain "He loves me, he loves me not . . ." as she picked the petals from a daisy. The Ox-eye Daisy is the very common, attractive, white and yellow daisy of fields. It can produce an undesirable flavor in the milk of cows that graze on it. It is the state flower of North Carolina. Introduced from Europe.

Range Naturalized throughout the state.

Habitat Open fields, roadsides, and other disturbed areas.

Blooming Period June–October.

Large-flowered Bellwort
(Uvularia grandiflora)
Lily Family (Liliaceae)

Day-lily
(Hemerocallis fulva)
Lily Family (Liliaceae)

Tiger Lily
(Lilium lancifolium)
Lily Family (Liliaceae)

Cindy Tucci

Description Drooping, bell-shaped yellow flower, 1½" long, growing at the end of an arching branch. Leaves appear to be pierced by the stem. Leaves have white hairs on lower side. Height: 6–20".

Comments Perennial. The genus is named for the drooping appearance of the flowers which resembles the uvula, the pendent fleshy lobe at the rear of the soft palate. The leaves which have not fully unfurled at flowering time give a wilted appearance, even though the plant is perfectly healthy. It favors a shady woods and is not sun-tolerant. Clearing its woodland habitat most likely will eliminate the Bellwort. Native.

Range Throughout the state.

Habitat In calcareous soil of rich woods.

Blooming Period April–June.

Desription Large orange, funnel-shaped flower, 3–4" wide, facing upward. Flowers in a terminal cluster on a bare stem. Only one or two flowers will bloom at a time. Individual flowers are open for only one day. Leaves linear, all basal, up to 2 Ft. long. Height: 3–6 ft.

Comments Perennial. The plant does not produce fertile seeds, but reproduces vegetatively from the roots. English colonists planted them in their gardens. Day-lilies have escaped from cultivation and are now naturalized as wildflowers. Introduced from Eurasia.

Range Abundant throughout the state.

Habitat Roadsides and sites of old homesteads.

Blooming Period June–August.

Desription Orange flower with brown spots, 3–4" wide, with 6 recurved petals. Distinctive black bulblets in axils of leaves. Leaves alternate, narrow. Upper stem covered with dense, white hairs. Height: 3–5 ft.

Comments Perennial. The strikingly beautiful flowers bloom for only a single day. The dense white hairs which cover the upper stem are described as resembling a cobweb. This very hardy lily has escaped from cultivation. It is similar to the rare Turk's-cap Lily (*L. superbum*), which lacks the black bulblets in the leaf axils. Introduced from Asia.

Range Naturalized at scattered sites throughout the state.

Habitat Old homesites and roadsides.

Blooming Period July–August.

Canada Lily
(Lilium canadense)
Lily Family (Liliaceae)

Michigan Lily
(Lilium michiganense)
Lily Family (Liliaceae)

Yellow Trout-lily
(Erythronium americanum)
Lily Family (Liliaceae)

David Dister

Desription Orange (to red) distinctive nodding flowers, 2–3" long, with 3 petals and 3 sepals. Anthers brown. Leaves in whorls of 4–10 on the stem. Stem slender, smooth. Height: 2–5 ft.

Comments Perennial. The flowers grow in terminal clusters of one to twelve blossoms. From the ends of long stalks, the flowers hang like bells. They are pollinated by butterflies, honeybees, and leaf-cutting bees. The plants often cluster in large groups in moist areas. Early Native Americans collected the flower buds and roots for food. Native.

Range Eastern and southern counties of the state.

Habitat Acid to neutral soils of moist meadows, swamps, and streamsides.

Blooming Period June–August.

Desription Orange flower, 3" wide, with 3 petals and 3 sepals recurved with their tips nearly touching. Each flower on a separate stalk or branch. Leaves whorled. Stem smooth. Height: 2–5 ft.

Comments Perennial. Look for a light green streak on the inside of the petals and sepals that forms a star inside the flower. This lily is closely related to the Turk's-cap Lily (*L. superbum*), which is rare, growing only in a few northeastern and southern counties. Native.

Range Northwestern and western counties of the state.

Habitat Moist woodland borders, streambanks, wet meadows, and roadside ditches.

Blooming Period June–July.

Desription Solitary yellow nodding flower, ¾–1½" long, composed of 3 petals and 3 sepals, slightly reflexed. 1 pair of smooth, somewhat fleshy, mottled leaves 3–8" long. Height: 4–10".

Comments Perennial. The common name refers to the mottled leaves, which resemble the color pattern of a fawn or brook trout. Also called Yellow Fawn-lily and Dog-tooth Violet (not a true violet). The leaves and flower stalk grow from bulbs growing 6–15" deep in the soil. For 2–3 years, the plant grows as a small, single leaf. From 4–6 years, the plant grows as larger, single leaves. Finally, after 6–7 years, the plant sends up large, double leaves and the flower. This beautiful wildflower grows in extensive colonies of hundreds of plants. Native.

Range Widely distributed in the state.

Habitat Moist woods.

Blooming Period March–May.

Yellow Iris
(Iris pseudacorus)
Iris Family (Iridaceae)

Yellow Lady's-slipper
(Cypripedium calceolus)
Orchid Family (Orchidaceae)

Lesser Celandine
(Ranunculus ficaria)
Buttercup Family (Ranunculaceae)

Cindy Tucci

Desription Showy, bright yellow flower, 3–4" wide, in branched clusters. Petals 3 and sepals 3. Leaves basal, sword-like, taller than the stem. Stem stout. Height: 2–3 ft.

Comments Perennial. Also known as Yellow Water-flag. This is the only yellow iris to be found growing in the wild. Look for this stately plant growing in clumps in standing water. Moisture and light are two environmental conditions for lush plant growth. Both conditions are abundant in wet areas where plants are characteristically tall. Plants of wet habitats devote much energy toward the growth of stems and leaves. It has escaped from cultivation, and is now established as a wildflower. A species of Iris is the state flower of Tennessee. Introduced from Europe.

Range Scattered throughout the state.

Habitat Swamps, shallow water along streams and ponds, and wet roadside ditches.

Blooming Period May–June.

Description Yellow flower with inflated lip (the "slipper"), 2" long. Petals 2 and sepals 2, twisted spirally, greenish-brown at the side. Leaves oval-shaped, with dark veins. Height: 1–2 ft.

Comments Perennial. The species name comes from the Latin word meaning "little shoe." These beautiful wildflowers grow in the humus-covered ground of old, stable woodlands. The excitement which occurs at the discovery of a Lady's-slipper is unparalleled. Yellow Lady's-slipper is a potentially threatened species. They will not survive transplanting and should be left undisturbed in their existing location. Native.

Range At scattered sites in the northeastern and southern counties of the state.

Habitat Calcareous soil of rich moist woods, swamps, and bogs.

Blooming Period May–July.

Description Yellow flower, 1" wide, with 8–12 shiny petals and 3–4 green sepals. Stamens numerous. Leaves heart-shaped, long-stalked, bluntly toothed. Height: 2–6".

Comments Perennial. The bright and showy petals attract many insects. The petals glisten as if waxed. This is a low plant of wet places, but not submerged. It is similar to Marsh Marigold (*Caltha palustris*), which has 5–9 yellow petal-like sepals, is taller, and has roots submerged. Introduced from Europe, where it commonly grows in pastures.

Range Throughout the state.

Habitat Streambanks, floodplains, gardens, and dry ground with damp shade.

Blooming Period April–May.

Kidney-leaf Buttercup
(Ranunculus abortivus)
Buttercup Family (Ranunculaceae)

Hispid Buttercup
(Ranunculus hispidus)
Buttercup Family (Ranunculaceae)

Marsh Marigold
(Caltha palustris)
Buttercup Family (Ranunculaceae)

Description Yellow flower, ⅓" wide, with 5–7 petals. Stem leaves alternate and deeply divided. Basal leaves have kidney-shaped blades. Stem smooth. Height: 6–24".

Comments Also known as Small-flowered Buttercup. Close examination reveals the numerous stamens, characteristic of the Buttercup Family. In many places this plant is regarded merely as a weed. Native.

Range Throughout the state.

Habitat Woods and moist ground.

Blooming Period April–August.

Description Yellow flower, 1" wide, with 5 glossy petals. Stamens numerous. Compound leaves with 3 leaflets. Stem erect, very hairy. Height: 1–2 ft.

Comments Perennial. The species name comes from the Latin (*hispidus*) meaning rough or covered with bristles, which describes the hairy stems. All buttercups are pollinated by flies and bees. Native.

Range At scattered sites throughout the state.

Habitat Moist woods and thickets, streambanks, and floodplains.

Blooming Period March–May.

Description Bright yellow flower, 1½" wide, with 5–9 petal-like sepals. Stamens numerous. Leaves dark green, glossy, round or kidney-shaped, and long-stalked. Stem thick, succulent, and hollow. Height: 1–2 ft.

Comments Perennial. Also known as Cowslip. The family name comes from the Latin (*ranunculus*) meaning "little frog." This is in reference to its wet habitat, where frogs are likely to be found. It resembles large Buttercups, rather than Marigolds. The flowers are pollinated by bees which see in ultraviolet wave lengths as well as visible light. These flowers, which appear uniformly yellow to human eyes, have distinct patterns of nectar guides, which are visible only under the sun's ultraviolet light, thus attracting bees. It is exciting to discover a colony of this bright, early spring wildflower. Native.

Range At selected sites throughout the state.

Habitat Swamps, marshes, streamsides, and other wet areas.

Blooming Period April–June.

Celandine-poppy
(Stylophorum diphyllum)
Poppy Family (Papaveraceae)

Yellow Corydalis
(Corydalis flavula)
Poppy Family (Papaveraceae)

Black Mustard
(Brassica nigra)
Mustard Family (Brassicaceae)

Description Bright yellow flowers, 1–2" wide, with 4 petals. Leaves 1 pair, deeply lobed. Other leaves are basal. Stem with yellow juice. Height: 10–16".

Comments Perennial. Also known as Wood-poppy. The species name comes from the Greek (*di* and *phyllum*) meaning "two leaves." The fruit is a green oval capsule that is bristly and hairy. Native.

Range Mostly in the eastern and southern counties of the state.

Habitat Rich moist woods, wooded flood-plains, and moist cliffs.

Blooming Period March–May.

Description Pale yellow flowers, ½" long, growing in a raceme. Upper lip forms a toothed crest. Spur short, only on the upper side. Leaves bluish-green, finely divided. Stem delicate. Height: 6–16".

Comments Annual. The genus name is very fitting, coming from the Greek meaning "crested lark." The beauty of this delicate flower can be appreciated even more with the aid of a hand lens. Native.

Range Infrequent. Only at scattered sites throughout the state.

Habitat Rocky slopes, gravel banks, and open sandy woods.

Blooming Period April–May.

Description Yellow flower, ⅓" wide, with 4 petals, growing in a terminal cluster. Seed pods hug the stem. Upper leaves lance-shaped, hairless. Lower leaves coarsely lobed and bristly. Stem thick, bristly with sharp hairs, especially on the lower parts. Height: 2–7 ft.

Comments Annual. The alternative family name, Cruciferae, refers to the petals, which form a cross. The seeds, which are used in the preparation of table mustard, yield a glucoside (sinigrin) that gives the odor and flavor to this condiment. It is a close relative of cabbages, broccoli, and turnips. This plant is a serious "weed" throughout Ohio's farmlands. Introduced from Europe.

Range Throughout the state.

Habitat Cultivated fields, roadsides, and disturbed areas.

Blooming Period June–October.

Winter Cress
(Barbarea vulgaris)
Mustard Family (Brassicaceae)

Rough-fruited Cinquefoil
(Potentilla recta)
Rose Family (Rosaceae)

Common Cinquefoil
(Potentilla simplex)
Rose Family (Rosaceae)

Description Bright yellow flowers, ½" wide, with 4 petals, growing in clusters at the top of the stem. Upper leaves somewhat clasping the stem. Basal leaves with rounded "ears." Height: 1–2 ft.

Comments Biennial. Also known as Yellow Rocket Mustard. The young leaves can be used in salads, either cooked, or as greens. Introduced from Europe.

Range Common throughout the state.

Habitat Gardens, cultivated fields, roadsides, and disturbed areas.

Blooming Period April–August.

Description Pale yellow flower, ½–¾" wide, with 5 petals. A rounded notch at the tip of the petals. Leaves with 5–7 leaflets, toothed, and hairy. Stem erect, hairy. Height: 1–2 ft.

Comments Perennial. The flowers appear to have 10 sepals; however, the outer 5 are actually bracts. With a hand lens, observe the the stamens and pistils which are growing on a central dome. Introduced from Europe.

Range Rapidly spreading throughout the state.

Habitat Roadsides, dry fields, and disturbed habitats.

Blooming Period June–August.

Description Yellow flower, ½" wide, with 5 petals, growing on long stalks. Flowers and leaves on separate stalks. Leaves palmately compound, with 5 toothed leaflets.

Comments Perennial. Common name comes from the Latin (*quinque folia*) meaning five leaves, in reference to the 5 leaflets. Also known as Five-fingers. The stems grow flat along the ground. The plant spreads by means of runners, 6–20" long. Native.

Range Throughout the state.

Habitat Fields and dry woods.

Blooming Period April–June.

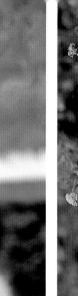

Yellow Sweet Clover
(Melilotus officinalis)
Pea Family (Fabaceae)

Hop Clover
(Trifolium aureum)
Pea Family (Fabaceae)

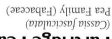

Partridge Pea
(Cassia fasciculata)
Pea Family (Fabaceae)

Description Showy yellow flower, 1" wide, with 5 petals, growing only in the leaf axils. Stamens 10: 4 yellow, 6 purple and drooping. Leaves pinnately compound with 8–15 pairs of small, narrow leaflets. Height: 1–3 ft.

Comments Annual. The leaflets are somewhat sensitive to the touch; that is, they tend to fold up after being touched or squeezed. As a member of the Pea Family, this plant serves to enrich the soil with much-needed nitrogen. Native.

Range Scattered throughout the state.

Habitat Sandy soil, old fields, roadsides, and railways.

Blooming Period July–September.

Description Yellow flower heads, ½" long, on an erect stalk. Leaflets nearly stalkless. Withered flower heads turn brown and persist as seeds mature. Stems smooth and erect. Height: 6–16".

Comments Annual. Fabaceae is a large and important family which is exceeded in diversity only by the Asteraceae. Examples of important agricultural members include peas, beans, soybeans, and peanuts. Hop Clover serves to prevent soil erosion, and enriches the soil because of its nitrogen-fixing nodules in the roots. It is similar to Black Medic (*Medicago lupulina*), which has smaller flowers, distinctive black seeds, and is usually prostrate. Introduced from Europe.

Range Throughout the state.

Habitat Lawns, gardens, roadsides, and other disturbed areas.

Blooming Period May–September.

Description Yellow flowers in a spike, 2–4" long. Leaves with 3 leaflets. Sweet odor when crushed. Height: 3–8 ft.

Comments Biennial. This plant is widely used as a cover crop in pastures because it harbors nitrogen-fixing bacteria in its root nodules, and thus enriches the soil as well as anchors it. Honeybees are frequent pollinators of the flowers. It provides cover for wildlife, though at the expense of plant diversity. It is similar to White Sweet Clover (*M. alba*), which has white flowers. Introduced from Eurasia.

Range Widespread throughout the state.

Habitat In calcareous soils of roadsides, field edges, and disturbed areas.

Blooming Period June–August.

Spotted Touch-me-not
(Impatiens capensis)
Touch-me-not Family (Balsaminaceae)

Yellow Wood-sorrel
(Oxalis stricta)
Wood-sorrel Family (Oxalidaceae)

Bird's-foot Trefoil
(Lotus corniculatus)
Pea Family (Fabaceae)

Description Bright yellow flowers, ½" wide, growing in a cluster of 3–6 at the ends of the branches. Compound leaf has 5 leaflets; 3 at the end of a stalk-like midrib, and 2 at the base resembling stipules. Height: 6–24".

Comments Perennial. The seed pods radiate from a central point, suggesting a bird's foot. This showy plant serves as food for wild animals, especially deer. Introduced from Europe.

Range Scattered throughout the state.

Habitat Fields, roadsides, and disturbed areas.

Blooming Period June–September.

Description Yellow flower, ½" wide; with 5 petals. Leaves divided into 3 heart-shaped, clover-like leaflets. Seed pods erect. Stem erect. Height: 6–15".

Comments Perennial. Also known as Sourgrass in reference to the sour taste of the leaves, which contain oxalic acid. The genus name comes from the Greek (*oxys*) meaning "sour." It is a common garden weed. Native.

Range Widespread throughout the state.

Habitat Woods, fields, roadsides, and disturbed areas.

Blooming Period June–October.

Description Orange flower, with red spots, 1" long, dangling from a long stalk. Flower composed of 1 large bell-shaped sepal, which extends horizontally and has a tail-like spur which curves underneath and parallel to the flower. Leaves ovate, thin, and bluntly toothed. Height: 2–5 ft.

Comments Annual. The common name refers to the ripe seed pods, which will explode at the slightest touch and shoot their seeds out at a distance of several feet. Also known as Jewelweed, because leaves appear silver when placed under water. The unusually shaped flower is especially adapted for pollination by hummingbirds, bees, and butterflies. It is more frequent than the Pale Touch-me-not (*I. pallida*); however, both species are occasionally seen growing side by side. Native.

Range Throughout the state.

Habitat Wet woodland borders, shaded riverbanks, and roadside ditches.

Blooming Period June–September.

Common St. Johnswort
(Hypericum perforatum)
St. Johnswort Family (Clusiaceae)

Flower-of-an-hour
(Hibiscus trionum)
Mallow Family (Malvaceae)

Pale Touch-me-not
(Impatiens pallida)
Touch-me-not Family (Balsaminaceae)

Description Yellow flower, 1" long, dangling from a long stalk. Flower composed of 1 large bell-like sepal which extends horizontally and has a tail-like spur that curves at right angle to the flower. Leaves ovate, thin, and bluntly toothed. Fruit at maturity is a swollen capsule which, when touched, will explode, expelling seeds up to 5 ft. away. Stem succulent. Height: 3–5 ft.

Comments Annual. Also known as Jewelweed. The juice from a crushed stem, when applied to the skin, will relieve the burning sensation from Wood Nettle (*Laportea canadensis*), which often grows in dense numbers near Touch-me-nots. It is commonly pollinated by Spicebush Swallowtail butterflies, bumblebees, and hummingbirds, as they feed on the nectar which is stored in the spur. Native.

Range Frequent in the eastern half of the state; less frequent westward.

Habitat Moist, shady ditches, streambanks, and woodland borders.

Blooming Period June–September.

Description Pale yellow flower, 1–2½" wide, with a purple eye. The flowers remain open only a few hours. Leaves deeply divided into 3–5 segments, which are coarsely toothed. Stems hairy. Height: 1–2 ft.

Comments Annual. This low, spreading plant is an attractive but unwelcome weed in cultivated fields and gardens. The flower opens in the morning but closes soon after the full sun reaches the plant. Introduced from Eurasia.

Range Naturalized throughout the state.

Habitat Open fields, railways, and disturbed areas.

Blooming Period June–September.

Description Yellow flowers, 1" wide, in clusters. Petals 5, with black dots along the margins. Stamens numerous. Leaves on branches are about ½ as long as leaves on the main stem. When held up to the light, translucent dots can be observed on the leaves. Stem is much-branched. Height: 1–3 ft.

Comments Perennial. The common name comes from the fact that the flowers supposedly begin to bloom on June 24, the eve of the birth of St. John the Baptist. For many years this herb has been used as an antidepressant. Introduced from Europe.

Range Throughout the state.

Habitat Roadsides, railways, dry fields, and disturbed areas.

Blooming Period June–September.

Golden Alexanders
(Zizia aurea)
Parsley Family (Apiaceae)

Common Evening-primrose
(Oenothera biennis)
Evening-primrose Family (Onagraceae)

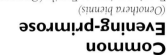

Downy Yellow Violet
(Viola pubescens)
Violet Family (Violaceae)

Description Yellow flower, ¾" wide. A leafy stem above the ground with the flower in the leaf axil. Hairy stem is distinctive. Leaves hairy beneath, broadly triangular. No basal leaves. Height: 6–16".

Comments Perennial. All violets have 5 petals: 2 at the top, 2 side "wings," and a lower petal that often serves as a landing place for insects seeking nectar. After the yellow flowers have been produced, cleistogamous flowers form near the base of the plant. These flowers never open and are self-fertilized. Native.

Range Throughout the state.

Habitat Moist to dry woodlands.

Blooming Period April–May.

Description Yellow flower, 1–2" wide, with cross-shaped stigma. Sepals reflexed. Flowers open by twilight, close by noon. Leaves lance-shaped, slightly toothed. Stem slightly red-tinged. Height: 1–6 ft.

Comments Biennial. The species name means biennial. Basal leaves become established the first year, and flowering occurs the second year. Soon after opening in the evening, the flowers are visited by hawk moths in search of nectar; thus the flower is pollinated. Native.

Range Throughout the state.

Habitat Dry, open fields, roadsides, and disturbed areas.

Blooming Period July–October.

Description Bright yellow flowers, 1½–2" wide, growing in an umbel. Leaves twice compound: 3 divisions are subdivided into 3 leaflets. Height: 1–3 ft.

Comments Perennial. The common name describes the bright color of the umbel. The species name comes from Latin (*aur*) for gold. The chemical symbol for gold is Au, and is number 79 on the periodic table of the elements. The double compound leaves are distinctive. When crushed, the leaves give off a strong parsley odor. It grows well in wet habitats. The plant is similar to Wild Parsnip (*Pastinaca sativa*), which is much taller, with larger umbels and pinnately compound leaves. Native.

Range Mainly in western counties of the state; however, scattered eastward.

Habitat Moist woods, thickets, swamps, and floodplains.

Blooming Period May–June.

Yellow Pimpernel
(Taenidia integerrima)
Parsley Family (Apiaceae)

Wild Parsnip
(Pastinaca sativa)
Parsley Family (Apiaceae)

Moneywort
(Lysimachia nummularia)
Primrose Family (Primulaceae)

Description Tiny yellow flowers growing in a delicate umbel, 3" wide, with long, slender rays. Leaves 2–3 times compound. Leaflets oval with smooth margins. Stem erect, slender, smooth. Height: 1–3 ft.

Comments Perennial. The flower cluster resembles a delicate starburst. Early Native Americans and settlers mixed pimpernel roots with herbal medicines to give a pleasant aroma of celery. It somewhat resembles Golden Alexanders (*Zizia aurea*), which has sharp-toothed leaflets. Native.

Range Throughout the state.

Habitat Dry woods, thickets, rocky hillsides, and roadside banks.

Blooming Period May–June.

Description Yellow flowers growing in umbels, 2–6" wide. Leaves divided into 5–15 sharply toothed leaflets. Stem stout, deeply grooved, and hairy. Height: 2–5 ft.

Comments Biennial. This coarse plant persists throughout the summer. Look for the leaf stalks which clasp the stem. The cultivated variety of this plant has a large, edible root. Introduced from Europe.

Range Naturalized throughout the state.

Habitat Roadsides, railways, abandoned fields, and other disturbed areas.

Blooming Period May–September.

Description Yellow flower, ¾" wide, with 5 petals, growing on long stalks growing in the axils of leaves. Leaves roundish, opposite. Stem, creeping: 6–24" long.

Comments Perennial. Moneywort forms showy mats when its flowers are in bloom. The species name is from the Latin (*nummus*) meaning "a coin" and refers to the shape of the leaves. Introduced from Europe.

Range Naturalized throughout the state.

Habitat Stream and lake margins, wet ditches, lawns, and disturbed, moist areas.

Blooming Period May–August.

Whorled Loosestrife

(Lysimachia quadrifolia)
Primose Family (Primulaceae)

Butterfly-weed

(Asclepias tuberosa)
Milkweed Family (Asclepiadaceae)

Hairy Puccoon

(Lithospermum caroliniense)
Borage Family (Boraginaceae)

Description Yellow flowers, ½" wide, with 5 petals, red ring near the center, growing on long stalks in the leaf axils. Flowers and leaves in distinctive whorls of 4 (variable). Height: 1–3 ft.

Comments Perennial. The genus is named for Lysimachus, the king of ancient Greece from 306–281 B.C. The species name is from Latin (*quad* and *folium*) meaning "four leaves" in reference to the number of leaves usually found in the whorl. Pollination is carried out by honeybees and bumblebees in search of nectar. It is similar to Fringed Loosestrife (*L. ciliata*), which has opposite leaves with petioles fringed with hairs. Native.

Range Common in the eastern and southern counties, and the Oak Openings area in extreme northwestern Ohio.

Habitat Open woods, thickets, sandy soil, and roadsides.

Blooming Period June–July.

Description Bright orange flowers growing in umbels, 2–3" wide. Individual flowers have 5 curved-back petals with a central crown. Leaves alternate, narrow. The only milkweed with alternate leaves and colorless juice. Stem stout and hairy. Height: 1–2 ft.

Comments Perennial. These brilliant flowers attract butterflies, which pollinate the flowers as they search for nectar as food. In the autumn, the narrow seed pods burst open and release numerous brown seeds with silky hairs, which are dispersed by the wind. Native.

Range Common in eastern and southern counties, then scattered throughout the remainder of the state.

Habitat Dry fields, hillsides, and roadsides.

Blooming Period June–September.

Description Yellow (to orange) flowers, 1" wide, tube-shaped, with 5 flaring lobes. Flower tube hairy inside at the base. Leaves alternate, numerous. Stem much branched. Stem and leaves with stiff, spreading hairs. Height: 1–2 ft.

Comments Perennial. This family of flowers is also known as the Forget-me-not Family. They are herbs usually covered with bristly hairs. The name "puccoon" is an early Native American name for several plants used for colored dyes. The clusters of Hairy Puccoon's bright flowers will catch your eye from a distance. It is similar to Hoary Puccoon (*L. canescens*), which is found in the southern half of Ohio and blooms earlier in the spring. Native.

Range Northern counties.

Habitat Dry woods and open sandy areas.

Blooming Period May–July.

Clammy Ground-cherry
(Physalis heterophylla)
Nightshade Family (Solanaceae)

Common Mullein
(Verbascum thapsus)
Snapdragon Family (Scrophulariaceae)

Butter-and-eggs
(Linaria vulgaris)
Snapdragon Family (Scrophulariaceae)

Description Yellow (to greenish-yellow) flower, ¾" wide, nodding, bell-shaped with a purple center. Leaves alternate, egg-shaped, slightly toothed. Stem sticky and hairy. Height: 1–3 ft.

Comments Perennial. The fruit is a yellow berry, the "cherry," enclosed in a thin paper-like husk. Native Americans and early settlers made preserves and pies from the ripe berries. Birds and wild animals feed on the fruit in the autumn. It is similar to Chinese Lantern (*P. alkekengi*), which is a cultivated garden variety with orange berries. Native.

Range Throughout the state.

Habitat Woodland borders, fields, pastures, railways, and roadsides.

Blooming Period June–September.

Description Yellow flowers, ¾–1" wide, growing in a dense spike. Only a few flowers are open at any time, thus giving the spike a ragged appearance. Leaves soft and velvety. Single thick stem. Height: 2–7 ft.

Comments Biennial. Tiny hairs cover the leaves and stem, making it look and feel like velvet. It forms a velvety-leaved basal rosette the first year and an erect flowering stem the year following. Native Americans and early settlers lined their boots with Mullein leaves for insulation. Introduced from Europe.

Range Naturalized throughout the state.

Habitat Stony hillsides, dry fields, roadsides, railways, and disturbed areas.

Blooming Period June–September.

Description Yellow flowers, 1" long, growing in a terminal cluster. Upper lip 2-lobed. Lower lip 3-lobed, with orange ridges and a nectar spur at the base. Leaves very narrow and numerous. Height: 1–3 ft.

Comments Perennial. It is related to the garden snapdragon and will open its "mouth" when squeezed. The weight of a bee alighting on the lower lip will open the flower so that the bee can enter to feed on the nectar. The bee emerges covered with pollen, then flies from flower to flower, thus cross-pollinating the flowers. The underground rhizomes grow deep and are thus protected from drought and physical damage. Introduced from Europe.

Range Naturalized throughout the state.

Habitat Dry fields, railways, roadsides, and disturbed areas.

Blooming Period June–October.

Downy False Foxglove

(Aureolaria virginica)
Snapdragon Family (Scrophulariaceae)

Stiff Goldenrod

(Solidago rigida)
Aster Family (Asteraceae)

Flat-topped Goldenrod

(Solidago graminifolia)
Aster Family (Asteraceae)

Description Yellow flowers, 1–1½" long, trumpet-shaped with 5 lobes, growing in pairs in axils of upper leaves. Leaves opposite, bluntly lobed, downy. Stem downy. Height: 2–4 ft.

Comments Perennial. The common name refers to the fine hairs (down) that cover the leaves and stem. Close examination of the flower reveals the throat to be lined with hairs. All members of *Aureolaria* are semiparasitic on the roots of oak trees. True Foxgloves are in the genus *Digitalis*. Native.

Range Eastern half of the state.

Habitat Sandy, acid soil. Dry open woodlands.

Blooming Period June–September.

Description Yellow flowers growing in an umbel, 5–6" wide. Distinctive leaves opposite, oval, rigid, and rough textured. Stem hairy. Height: 1–5 ft.

Comments Perennial. The common and species names come from the Latin (*rigidus*) meaning "to be stiff" and refers to the firmness of the leaves. In early times it invaded overgrazed prairies in great numbers. Native.

Range Limited to certain sites throughout the state.

Habitat Sandy soils of prairies and prairie openings.

Blooming Period August–October.

Description Yellow flowers, growing in a flat-topped inflorescence. Leaves narrow, ¼" wide, rough, smooth margin, and 3–5 parallel veins. Stem smooth. Height: 2–4 ft.

Comments Perennial. Also known as Lance-leaved Goldenrod and Grass-leaved Goldenrod. The species name comes from the Latin (*gramini*) "grass" and (*folium*) "leaf." The flat-topped floral arrangement and narrow leaves are distinctive. Native.

Range Very common and widely distributed in the state.

Habitat Moist fields, thickets, roadsides, and streambanks.

Blooming Period August–October.

Zigzag Goldenrod
(Solidago flexicaulis)
Aster Family (Asteraceae)

Blue-stem Goldenrod
(Solidago caesia)
Aster Family (Asteraceae)

Gray Goldenrod
(Solidago nemoralis)
Aster Family (Asteraceae)

Description Yellow flower clusters growing in the leaf axils. Leaves egg-shaped, broad, sharply toothed, and pointed at both ends. Stem distinctively zigzag. Height: 1–3 ft.

Comments Perennial. The species name comes from the Latin (*flex* and *caulis*) meaning "to bend" and "stem." Although not one of the more showy goldenrods, it gives the wildflower observer a sense of satisfaction to recognize this plant with its distinctive stem. Native.

Range Common throughout the state.

Habitat Rich woods.

Blooming Period August–October.

Description Yellow flowers growing in axils of reduced leaves. Leaves narrow, smooth, and toothed. Stem smooth, arching, and bluish due to a waxy surface. Height: 1–3 ft.

Comments Perennial. There are many kinds of goldenrods which look very much alike except for the shape, margin, veins, and arrangement of the leaves. The yellow disk and ray flowers of this species grow in small clusters. Sometimes the stem bends almost horizontal and forms a "wreath" with the series of flower clusters. Native.

Range Throughout the state.

Habitat Rich, open woodlands and thickets.

Blooming Period August–October.

Description Yellow flower cluster, slightly one-sided. Distinctive tiny leaflets in the axils of the leaves. Leaves gray and rough. Stem gray and densely covered with fine hairs. Height: 1–3 ft.

Comments Perennial. Goldenrods are perennial plants, growing from a spreading root system of rhizomes. Thus goldenrods often grow in large colonies. Many years ago, people thought that pollen from goldenrod was the cause of hay fever. Botanists have proven that hay fever is actually caused by pollen from ragweed and other wind-pollinated plants which bloom at the same time. Native.

Range Scarce in the west-central counties, otherwise common throughout the state.

Habitat Dry, open woodlands.

Blooming Period August–October.

Canada Goldenrod

(Solidago canadensis)
Aster Family (Asteraceae)

Cup-plant

(Silphium perfoliatum)
Aster Family (Asteraceae)

Prairie-dock

(Silphium terebinthinaceum)
Aster Family (Asteraceae)

Description Small yellow flower heads on outward-arching branches that form a pyramidal cluster. Leaves dense, 3-veined, narrow, lance-shaped, and sharply toothed. Leaves decrease gradually in size from the base of the plant upward. Stem downy at top, but smooth near the base. Height: 1–5 ft.

Comments Perennial. As it is with animals, so it is with plants: there is always a struggle for existence. Those best adapted to their environment will survive, while those less adapted fall by the wayside. The old adage that "in union there is strength" is proved by the goldenrods. The numerous flower heads grow so close together that when an insect simply crawls across the flower head it will pollinate large numbers of the flowers, thus assuring the production of sufficient numbers of seeds. Goldenrod is the state flower of Alabama, Kentucky, and Nebraska. Native.

Range Abundant throughout the state.
Habitat Fields, thickets, and roadsides.
Blooming Period August–September.

Description Yellow flower heads, 1–2" wide, with 20–30 rays. Leaves coarsely toothed, in pairs, and clasped with a cup around the stem. Stems smooth. Height: 4–8 ft.

Comments Perennial. Also known as dimple cup. The species name comes from the Latin *per* and *folium*, through the leaf, in reference to the stem appearing to grow directly through the leaves. The flowers resemble sunflowers. The prominent disk-shaped leaves which form a cup around the stem are no mistake, as many observers feel. The cups collect rain water which is used as emergency drinking water. Native.

Range Common throughout the state.
Habitat Moist woodlands, streambanks, and floodplains.
Blooming Period July–September.

Description Yellow flower, 2–3" wide, with 12–15 rays. Numerous flower heads present. Leaves basal, heart-shaped, long-stemmed, coarsely toothed, and very large: 1–2 ft. long. Height: 4–9 ft.

Comments Perennial. This species is a characteristic plant of prairies. The huge basal leaves are very obvious long before the stalks with flowers are produced. The leaves are as rough as sandpaper. As an adaptation to life on the hot, dry prairie, the enormous leaf blades grow in a vertical position, reducing direct contact with the sun's rays. This reduces evaporation and conserves water for the plant. The sap of the plant was used by early settlers as chewing gum. Native.

Range Common in the northern and northwestern counties. Otherwise scattered throughout the prairie openings of the state.
Habitat Prairies and prairie remnants.
Blooming Period August–September.

[handwritten margin note: leaf, prairie dock, compass 94]

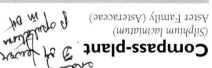

Compass-plant
(*Silphium laciniatum*)
Aster Family (Asteraceae)

Whorled Rosinweed
(*Silphium trifoliatum*)
Aster Family (Asteraceae)

Ox-eye
(*Heliopsis helianthoides*)
Aster Family (Asteraceae)

Description Yellow flowers, 3" wide, surrounded by hairy, green bracts. Leaves alternate, 12–18" long, deeply cleft, and very rough. Stem coarse. Height: 4–10 ft.

Comments Perennial. The common name refers to the leaves which orient themselves generally in a north-south direction. This plant has a taproot 6 ft. or more deep which is an adaptation for obtaining water in dry areas, and for surviving prairie fires. It is an endangered species and must be protected. Many nature centers are establishing Compass-plant to restored prairie openings in Ohio. Native.

Range Rare in Ohio. Only in selected prairie sites.

Habitat Prairies.

Blooming Period July–September

Description Yellow flower head, 1½–2" wide, with 15–20 rays. Similar to sunflowers. Leaves lance-shaped, in whorls of 3 (occasionally opposite or alternate). Leaves rough and coarsely toothed. Stem smooth. Height: 3–7 ft.

Comments Perennial. The species name comes from the Latin (*tri* and *folium*), meaning "three leaves," in reference to the whorls of 3 leaves. The stem branches at the top, producing several flower heads simultaneously. Flowers from this genus produce dry fruits (achenes), containing a single seed, only from the ray flowers. Native.

Range Scarce in the northwestern counties, but common in the remainder of the state.

Habitat Woodland borders, thickets, and prairies.

Blooming Period July–September.

Description Large yellow flower head, 1–2" wide, with 10 or more ray flowers. The distinctive ray flowers have a small forked stigma at the base (not present in true sunflowers). Disk yellow, cone-shaped. Leaves opposite, stalked, and toothed. Stem smooth. Height: 2–5 ft.

Comments Perennial. Ox-eye closely resembles sunflowers (*Helianthus*). Look for the tubular disk flowers with stamens and pistils. Unlike sunflowers and coneflowers, Ox-eye produces fertile seeds from the ray flowers. Native.

Range Throughout the state.

Habitat Moist soil, open woodlands, streambanks, floodplains, and prairies.

Blooming Period July–September.

Green-headed Coneflower
(Rudbeckia laciniata)
Aster Family (Asteraceae)

Black-eyed Susan
(Rudbeckia hirta)
Aster Family (Asteraceae)

Thin-leaved Coneflower
(Rudbeckia triloba)
Aster Family (Asteraceae)

Description Yellow flower head, 2–3" wide, with 6–10 drooping rays. Disk is a green knob. Upper leaves simple; lower leaves deeply cut with 3–5 pointed lobes. Stems highly branched, smooth. Height: 3–10 ft.

Comments Perennial. The leaves on this tall plant grow to be over 1 ft. wide. A cultivated variety with "double flowers" or extra ray flowers, known as Golden Glow, is sold commercially. The disk flowers have stamens and pistils which produce fertile seeds. The ray flowers are sterile. Native.

Range Locally abundant throughout the state.

Habitat Rich, moist ground, streambanks, and floodplains.

Blooming Period July–September.

Description Large daisy-like flower head, 2–3" wide, with 10–20 yellow rays. Disk chocolate-brown. The flower head is borne singly on a coarse, hairy stem. Leaves alternate, rough, and hairy. Height: 1–3 ft.

Comments Biennial. The Swedish botanist Carolus Linnaeus named the genus in honor of his botany professor, Olaf Rudbeck (1660–1740). Livestock usually avoid Black-eyed Susan, which can be toxic when eaten. Seeds of this popular wildflower can be purchased from commercial seed companies for planting in flower gardens. It forms a rosette the first year, and an erect flowering stem the year following. Black-eyed Susans originally were strictly prairie plants but now are common in most open fields. It is the state flower of Maryland. Native.

Range Common throughout the state.

Habitat Dry fields, roadsides, and open woods.

Blooming Period June–October.

Description Yellow flower head, 1–2" wide, with 8–10 ray flowers. Disk brown. Leaves alternate, rough on both sides. Lower leaves distinctively 3-lobed. Stem much branched, hairy. Height: 2–5 ft.

Comments Biennial. Look closely for the notch at the tip of the ray flowers. The highly branched stem produces several flowers simultaneously. The species name comes from the Greek (*trilobos*) meaning "three-lobed," referring to the 3-lobed leaves. Native.

Range Widespread throughout the state.

Habitat Open woods, thickets, and moist soil.

Blooming Period July–October.

Woodland Sunflower
(*Helianthus divaricatus*)
Aster Family (Asteraceae)

Hairy Sunflower
(*Helianthus mollis*)
Aster Family (Asteraceae)

Prairie Coneflower
(*Ratibida pinnata*)
Aster Family (Asteraceae)

Description Yellow ray flowers long, drooping. Disk egg-shaped, gray, becoming brown with age. Leaves compound, with 3–7 leaflets, lance-shaped, toothed. Stem hairy. Height: 3–5 ft.

Comments Perennial. Also known as Gray-headed Coneflower. When bruised, the disk and leaves give the scent of anise. The stem is branched at the top, producing several flower heads. Large colonies of Prairie Coneflowers often turn fields into a sea of yellow. Native.

Range At scattered sites throughout the state.

Habitat Common in calcareous soil. Prairies and prairie remnants, woodland borders, and railways.

Blooming Period July–October.

Description Yellow flower head, 2–3" wide, with 15–35 rays, disk yellow. Leaves opposite, sessile, gray-hairy. Stem gray-hairy. Height: 2–3 ft.

Comments Perennial. Also known as Ashy Sunflower due to the appearance of the dense gray hairs that cover the leaves and stem. This sunflower is highly nutritious and palatable to grazing animals. It is a threatened species because of its scarcity and must be protected. Native.

Range At prairie sites scattered throughout the state.

Habitat Prairies and dry soil of open woods and fields.

Blooming Period July–September.

Description Yellow flower head, 1–2" wide, with 8–15 ray flowers. Disk yellow. Leaves opposite, lance-shaped, rough, and toothed. Stalks of leaves less than ¼" or stalkless. Stem smooth below the flowers, but may become rough lower. Height: 2–6 ft.

Comments Perennial. The stem has many branches and produces several flowers simultaneously. The beauty of a field of sunflowers adds greatly to the spectacle of summer wildflowers. Sunflowers hybridize readily thus making identification sometimes difficult. Native.

Range Widely distributed throughout the state.

Habitat Dry woods, thickets, and roadsides.

Blooming Period July–October.

Wingstem
(*Verbesina alternifolia*)
Aster Family (Asteraceae)

Common Sunflower
(*Helianthus annuus*)
Aster Family (Asteraceae)

Jerusalem Artichoke
(*Helianthus tuberosus*)
Aster Family (Asteraceae)

Description Yellow flower, 2–3" wide, with 12–20 ray flowers. Disk yellow. Anthers form a brown tube around the style. Bracts of flower head long-pointed. Leaves broad, rough, winged stalks, and 3 main veins, usually white. Upper leaves alternate, lower leaves opposite. Stem rough, hairy, green or brown. Height: 6–10 ft.

Comments Perennial. "Jerusalem" is a corruption of the Italian (*girasole*, which means "turning to the sun"). Settlers boiled flower buds of edible sunflowers and ate them with butter as they did artichokes. This may have resulted in the name "Jerusalem Artichoke." The large tubers are edible, tasting much like potatoes. In their journal entry on April 9, 1805, Lewis and Clark described eating tubers prepared by their guide, Sacajawea. It is related to the Common Sunflower (*H. annuus*). Native.

Range Widely distributed throughout the state.

Habitat Moist soil along fencerows, ditches, streambanks, roadsides, and fields.

Blooming Period August–October.

Description Solitary large yellow sunflower, 3–6" wide, with brown disk. Leaves alternate, spade-shaped, rough, and toothed. Stem rough, hairy. Height: 3–12 ft.

Comments Annual. The genus name is derived from the Greek (*helios*, "sun," and *anthos*, "flower"). Throughout the day, the flowers follow the sun from east to west. This plant is the smaller, wild variation of the cultivated giant garden sunflower. It was commonly used as flour for bread by Native Americans before European settlers arrived. The seeds are used commercially for human consumption, and for wild birdseed; they are especially attractive to Cardinals. This is the state flower of Kansas. Native to the western states, and escaped from cultivation.

Range Widely distributed throughout the state.

Habitat Fields, roadsides, and disturbed areas.

Blooming Period July–September.

Description Yellow flower heads, 1–2" wide, with 2–8 ray flowers drooping from a mop-like yellow disk. Leaves alternate, with margins running down to the distinctive "wings" on the stems. Height: 3–8 ft.

Comments Perennial. The distinctive flowers and winged stem are the keys to identifying this late summer wildflower. The flower appears to be stressed, but this is the natural growth. The winged stems persist throughout the winter and are present on the new plants in the spring long before the flowers appear. Native.

Range Common throughout the state.

Habitat Rich soil, woods edges, floodplains, and thickets near streams.

Blooming Period August–October.

Tall Coreopsis
(Coreopsis tripteris)
Aster Family (Asteraceae)

Tickseed Sunflower
(Bidens coronata)
Aster Family (Asteraceae)

Pineapple-weed
(Matricaria matricarioides)
Aster Family (Asteraceae)

Description Showy yellow flower heads, 2–2½" wide, with yellow disks, turning dark with age. Ray flowers with round tips. Leaves opposite, with 3 leaflets. Stem smooth, much-branched, producing numerous flower heads. Height: 3–9 ft.

Comments Perennial. Also known as Tickseed. The genus name comes from the Greek (*kore* and *opsis*) meaning "shaped like a bug" in reference to the shape of the seed. The species name comes from the Greek (*tri* and *pteron*) meaning "3-wing," in reference to the 3 leaflets. Native.

Range Throughout the state.

Habitat Woodland borders and thickets.

Blooming Period July–September.

Description Bright yellow flower head, 2" wide, with 6–10 rays. Disk yellow. Leaves opposite, deeply divided, and toothed. Stems leafy and much-branched, bearing several flower heads. Height: 2–5 ft.

Comments Annual or Biennial. The genus name comes from Latin (*bi* and *dens*) meaning "two teeth" referring to the 2 strong spines of the seed that stick to animal fur and clothing, thus aiding in seed dispersal. Native.

Range Widely distributed throughout the state.

Habitat Wet meadows, roadside ditches, floodplains, and other wet areas.

Blooming Period August–October.

Description Yellow flowers in dome-shaped heads, ¼" wide, at the ends of branches. Stems very leafy. Leaves finely dissected. A low, sprawling plant. Height: 6–18".

Comments Annual. When crushed, flower heads give the odor of fresh pineapple. A common weedy species of rather sterile habitats. Introduced from western United States.

Range Common throughout the state.

Habitat Roadsides, barnyards, and other disturbed areas.

Blooming Period June–October.

Tansy

(Tanacetum vulgare)
Aster Family (Asteraceae)

Coltsfoot

(Tussilago farfara)
Aster Family (Asteraceae)

Butterweed

(Senecio glabellus)
Aster Family (Asteraceae)

Jeanne Willis

Description Numerous yellow flowers in a dense, flat-topped cluster of buttonlike heads without ray flowers. Leaves alternate, deeply cut, finely divided, and fern-like. Strongly aromatic. Height: 1–3 ft.

Comments Perennial. Tansy is very impressive with its bright yellow flowers in contrast with its dark green leaves. The leaves and stems contain tanacetic acid, which is toxic to humans and domestic animals. In early times it was cultivated for medicinal purposes. It has since escaped from gardens and is now well established as a wildflower. Introduced from Europe.

Range Naturalized throughout the state.

Habitat Roadsides, fields, old homesteads, and disturbed areas.

Blooming Period July–September.

Description Yellow dandelion-like flower, 1" wide, blooming in early spring. Flower stalk with reddish scales, grows upright from a horizontal rhizome. Flowers bloom before leaves appear. Basal leaves only, heart-shaped with shallow lobes, toothed, with long stems, and densely white woolly beneath. Height: 6–18".

Comments Perennial. There is only one species in the genus. The common name refers to the leaf resembling the shape of a colt's foot. Also known as Coughwort. The genus name comes from Latin (*tussis*) for "cough." Early settlers ground the leaves to make a cough remedy. The branching root system anchors soil on steep banks to prevent erosion. Introduced from Europe.

Range Well established in the eastern half of the state.

Habitat Wet clay soils of roadsides, railways, gravel banks, and other disturbed areas.

Blooming Period March–May.

Description Bright yellow flower heads, ½" wide, in dense clusters at the ends of branches. Individual flowers have 7–10 rays. Leaves alternate, coarsely toothed, with rounded lobes. Stem stout, fleshy, and hollow. Height: 2–3 ft.

Comments Annual. Also known as Yellowtop. Notice the leaves, which have a terminal lobe that is slightly larger than the other lobes. This plant has become a serious weed of many farms and gardens. Introduced from Europe.

Range Locally in southwestern Ohio, now spreading rapidly throughout the state.

Habitat Wet cultivated fields, roadsides, and disturbed areas.

Blooming Period May–July.

Golden Ragwort

(Senecio aureus)
Aster Family (Asteraceae)

Yellow Salsify

(Tragopogon dubius)
Aster Family (Asteraceae)

Yellow Goatsbeard

(Tragopogon pratensis)
Aster Family (Asteraceae)

Cindy Tucci

Description Yellow flowers growing in flat-topped clusters. Individual composite flower ½–¾" wide. Stem leaves deeply toothed. Basal leaves heart-shaped, long-stemmed, without winged petioles. Height: 1–3 ft.

Comments Perennial. This is a plant of wet habitats. It often grows in dense colonies. It is similar to Roundleaf Ragwort (*S. obovatus*), which has oval basal leaves with winged petioles. Native.

Range Common throughout the state.

Habitat Moist woods, swamps and wet meadows.

Blooming Period April–July.

Description Lemon-yellow flower head, 1–2" wide, on a tall stalk. Distinctive green bracts extend beyond the ray flowers. Flowers close by midday. Leaves long, linear, and grasslike. Stem smooth. Height: 2–3 ft.

Comments Biennial. When the flowers close, they form pointed cylinders. Later, the spherical ball of brown seeds opens. Each seed is attached to a parachute which aids in its dispersal by the wind. It is similar to Yellow Goatsbeard (*T. pratensis*), which has ray flowers longer than the bracts. Introduced from Europe.

Range Widely established throughout the state.

Habitat Meadows, fields, and roadsides.

Blooming Period June–August.

Description Yellow flower head, 1–2" wide, on long stalk. Ray flowers longer than the bracts. Flowers close at midday. Leaves grasslike, clasp the stem. Stem smooth. Juice milky. Height: 1–3 ft.

Comments Biennial. Its spherical puffball of seeds is similar to that of the Dandelion, but 2–3" wide. The seeds are attached to parachutes that assist in their dispersal by wind. Introduced from Europe.

Range Widely established throughout the state.

Habitat Fields, roadsides, and disturbed areas.

Blooming Period June–August.

Dandelion
(Taraxacum officinale)
Aster Family (Asteraceae)

Spiny-leaved Sow-thistle
(Sonchus asper)
Aster Family (Asteraceae)

Wild Lettuce
(Lactuca canadensis)
Aster Family (Asteraceae)

Description Yellow flower head, 1–2" wide, with 150–200 tiny flowers. Leaves with jagged lobes, resembling sharp teeth. Hollow stem produces milky sap. Height: 2–18".

Comments Perennial. The common name comes the French (*dent de lion*) meaning "lion's tooth," which describes the toothed margins of the leaves. Dandelions survive the winter by storing energy in the long, thick taproot. The same deep taproot enables the plant to survive conditions of drought. A fluffy ball of seeds, each with parachute-like hairs, is a favorite of children to blow, and help the wind disperse the seeds. The leaves may be eaten fresh or cooked. The stems are hollow, allowing them to bend without breaking under windy conditions. This same principle is used in the construction of flagpoles. Introduced from Europe.

Range Naturalized; occurring in every county of the state.

Habitat Lawns, fields, and disturbed areas.

Blooming Period March–December.

Description Pale yellow flower head, 1" wide. Leaves with numerous spiny teeth. Leaves with distinctive earlike lobes at the bases that are curled, clasping the stem. Stem grooved, hollow, with milky juice. Height: 1–5 ft.

Comments Annual. Sow-thistles are so common that they are often passed over as unattractive weeds. However, they are interesting plants to examine. The seeds are important food for birds. The seeds are dispersed by means of parachutes carried by the wind. Introduced from Europe.

Range Naturalized throughout the state.

Habitat Roadsides, fields, and disturbed areas.

Blooming Period July–October.

Description Pale yellow flower head, ¼" wide, growing in a large, loose cluster. Leaves prickly; variable in shape from deeply lobed to arrow-shaped, clasping and nearly entire. When broken, leaves and stem exude a milky juice. Stem smooth. Height: 3–10 ft.

Comments Biennial. The numerous flower heads grow upright on spreading branches that resemble a candelabra. The seeds are attached to parachutes which aid in their dispersal by wind. Native.

Range Throughout the state.

Habitat Fields, open woods, roadsides, fencerows, and disturbed areas.

Blooming Period June–September.

Orange Hawkweed
(Hieracium aurantiacum)
Aster Family (Asteraceae)

Rattlesnake Weed
(Hieracium venosum)
Aster Family (Asteraceae)

King Devil
(Hieracium caespitosum)
Aster Family (Asteraceae)

Description Orange flower head, ¾" wide, growing in a small cluster. Leaves hairy, only in a basal rosette. Stem hairy. Height: 1–2 ft.

Comments Perennial. Also known as Devil's Paintbrush. This plant belongs to a group of plants generally known as hawkweeds. There are 12 species of hawkweeds in Ohio. Seven of them are native. The native hawkweeds have leaves ascending the stem, whereas the alien species have leaves only in basal rosettes. The Orange Hawkweed was introduced from Europe.

Range Widely distributed throughout the eastern half of the state.

Habitat Dry fields, pastures, and roadsides.

Blooming Period June–September.

Description Bright yellow flower heads, ½" wide, growing on a tall, smooth stalk. Stem with small leaves. Basal leaves have distinctive reddish-purple veins. Height: 1–2 ft.

Comments Perennial. The common name originally referred to the plant growing in areas where rattlesnakes lived. The species name refers to the venom of rattlesnakes. Today the plant still exists, but the rattlesnakes are decreasing in numbers throughout the state. Native.

Range Eastern and southern counties of the state.

Habitat Open woods, woodland borders and clearings.

Blooming Period May–September.

Description Bright yellow flower heads, ½" wide, on a tall stalk. Basal leaves long, narrow, smooth-margined, and very hairy on both surfaces. Stem green, and very hairy. Height: 1–3 ft.

Comments Perennial. Also known as Field Hawkweed. All plants of the genus *Hieracium* can be called hawkweeds. In spite of being in the Aster Family, the flower heads are composed of only ray flowers without any disk flowers. They all have basal leaves that grow in a rosette which is flattened against the ground. Introduced from Europe.

Range Throughout the eastern half of the state, and scattered elsewhere.

Habitat Fields, pastures, and roadsides.

Blooming Period May–September.

Pink and Red *flowers*

Wild Garlic
(*Allium canadense*)
Lily Family (Liliaceae)

Field Garlic
(*Allium vineale*)
Lily Family (Liliaceae)

Flowering Rush
(*Butomus umbellatus*)
Flowering Rush Family (Butomaceae)

Description Pink flowers, ¾" wide, with 3 petals and 3 sepals, growing in large numbers at the top of a naked stalk. Leaves basal, grass-like. Stem smooth. Height: 2–3 ft.

Comments Perennial. This family has but a single genus and species. This tall herbaceous plant has migrated from the St. Lawrence River valley. The first specimens in Ohio were collected in 1936. It is spreading rapidly throughout many northern counties. It reproduces from grain-like tubers, which detach from thick rootstocks. Introduced from Eurasia.

Range Counties bordering Lake Erie.
Habitat Mudflats and shallow water.
Blooming Period June–August.

Description Red-purple (to pink, white, or greenish) flowers growing in an umbel, 1–2" wide. Often the many bulblets entirely replace the flowers in the umbel. Single spathe below the umbel. Leaves, grass-like, cylindrical, and hollow, ascend the stem partway. Height: 1–3 ft.

Comments Perennial. It has an edible bulb with a strong garlic taste. If the plants become too abundant in pastures, they result in an undesirable flavor to milk and butter. It is considered by many people to be an invasive, troublesome weed. It is related to the cultivated garlic (*A. sativum*). Introduced from Europe.

Range Naturalized throughout the state.
Habitat Fields, lawns, and gardens.
Blooming Period May–July.

Description Pink (to white) flowers growing in an erect cluster containing numerous small bulblets. Bulblets appear at the end of the erect stem and are more common than flowers. Leaves grass-like, flat, solid, and mostly near the base. Height: 8–24".

Comments Perennial. Due to the distinctive onion odor of a leaf when crushed, this plant is commonly called Wild Onion. The edible bulb has a pronounced onion taste. Native Americans harvested the bulbs as food throughout the year. It is related to the cultivated onion (*A. cepa*). Native.

Range Common and widespread throughout the state.
Habitat Moist woods, wooded floodplains, and moist meadows.
Blooming Period May–July.

Nodding Onion
(Allium cernuum)
Lily Family (Liliaceae)

Sessile Trillium
(Trillium sessile)
Lily Family (Liliaceae)

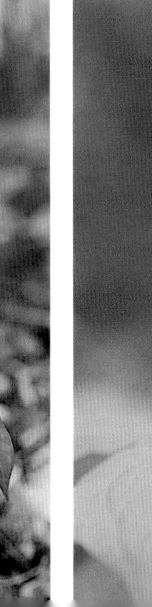

Red Trillium
(Trillium erectum)
Lily Family (Liliaceae)

Description Pale pink flowers growing in a distinctive nodding cluster on top of a single stalk. Leaves basal only, grass-like. Height: 1–2 ft.

Comments Perennial. When crushed, the leaves have a pronounced onion odor. The species name comes from the Latin (*cernuus*) meaning "falling forward" or "face down" referring to the position of the flowers. Native.

Range At scattered sites throughout the state.

Habitat Calcareous soil, gravel banks, prairie remnants, and roadsides.

Blooming Period July–August.

Description Maroon-red (also a yellowish-green form) flower, ¾–1" long, with 3 petals erect and sessile. Sepals 3. A whorl of 3 sessile leaves, mottled with light and dark green areas. Height: 4–12".

Comments Perennial. Also known as Toad-shade. The species is named for the flowers and leaves which are without stalks. Sessile Trilliums are usually found growing in large patches in the woods. They bloom early in the spring before the trees leaf out. Native.

Range Widespread in the state. Most frequent in the calcareous soils of the western counties.

Habitat Moist woods and thickets.

Blooming Period April–May.

Description Solitary, maroon-red flower, 2" wide, with distinctive unpleasant odor. Flower may be either erect or drooping. Petals 3, sepals 3, and leaves a whorl of 3. Height: 8–16".

Comments Perennial. Also known as Wake-robin or Stinking Benjamin. Its foul odor attracts carrion flies that act as pollinators. The petals are usually maroon in color; however, there are variations of white, yellow, and green. Regardless of the color, the petals always spread widely from the base to reveal the distinctive dark-colored ovary. Native.

Range Mostly in the eastern counties of the state.

Habitat Rich woods.

Blooming Period April–May.

Ken Hays

Showy Orchis
(Orchis spectabilis)
Orchid Family (Orchidaceae)

Jeanne Willis

Showy Lady's-slipper
(Cypripedium reginae)
Orchid Family (Orchidaceae)

David Dister

Pink Lady's-slipper
(Cypripedium acaule)
Orchid Family (Orchidaceae)

Description Solitary pink flower, 1–2" long. The slipper is usually reddish-pink with purple veins. Leaves 2, oval, basal. Stem naked. Height: 6–15".

Comments Perennial. Also known as Pink Moccasin Flower. This species is the only Lady's-slipper with no leaves on the flower stalk. This is one of the most beautiful wildflowers of late spring. Lady's-slippers will not survive transplanting, and therefore should be left undisturbed in their existing location. Native.

Range Northeastern and southern counties of the state.

Habitat In acid soil, sandy soil, dry pine or oak woods, and sometimes in bogs.

Blooming Period May–June.

Description A bi-colored flower (pink and white), 2 ½" wide. The slipper is usually reddish-pink with white streaks, but occasionally all purple. Leaves opposite, up to 10" long, growing from the flower stalk. Stem stout, hairy. Height: 1–2 ft.

Comments Perennial. Also known as the Queen Lady's-slipper. This is the largest and showiest of the Lady's-slippers. This beautiful orchid is a threatened species. It should be left undisturbed in its existing location because it will not survive transplanting. Overpicking has threatened the survival of the species. It is the state flower of Minnesota. Native.

Range Rare in Ohio. Found locally only in a few northern and central counties.

Habitat In limestone regions, wet woods, swamps, and bogs.

Blooming Period June–July.

Description Reddish-purple flowers (with white lower lip and spur), 1" long, growing in a loose spike of 2–10 flowers. Leaves 2, oval-shaped, smooth, basal. Stem rises between the 2 leaves. Height: 4–12".

Comments Perennial. The pink hood is formed from the sepals and lateral petals. As with most orchids, it will not survive transplanting, and should be left undisturbed in its existing location. Native.

Range Throughout the state.

Habitat Rich moist woods, especially beech-maple woods.

Blooming Period May–June.

Royal Catchfly
(*Silene regia*)
Pink Family (Caryophillaceae)

Wild Four-o'clock
(*Mirabilis nyctaginea*)
Four-o'clock Family (Nyctaginaceae)

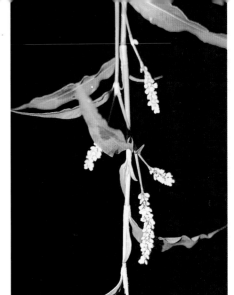

Lady's-thumb
(*Polygonum persicaria*)
Buckwheat Family (Polygonaceae)

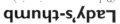

Jeanne Willis

Description Tiny pink flowers in spikes, 1" long. Leaves narrow, with a dark triangular spot near the middle. At every point where a leaf is attached to the stem, there is a tubular sheath. Top of sheath fringed with long hairs. Stem reddish. Height: 6–24".

Comments Annual. Also known as Smartweed. The common name refers to the dark spot on each leaf, resembling a bruise made by a "lady's thumb." In ancient times, many people believed that certain features of a plant were indications as to its medicinal use. This was known as the Doctrine of Signatures. Thus, Lady's Thumb was thought to have healing powers for bruises. It is similar to Pennsylvania Smartweed (*P. pensylvanicum*), which lacks the "thumb print" on the leaves and the fringe on the sheath. Introduced from Europe.

Range Abundant throughout the state.

Habitat Roadsides, damp clearings, cultivated fields, and other disturbed areas.

Blooming Period June–October.

Description Small pink or purple bell-shaped flowers, ¼" wide, in clusters of 2–5. Flowers open in late afternoon. A green star-shaped cup, ¾" wide, forms after flowering. Leaves opposite, heart-shaped. Smooth reddish stems are highly branched. Height: 1–5 ft.

Comments Perennial. Also known as Umbrella-wort. The flowers consist of a tubular calyx; there are no petals. It is closely related to the cultivated Four-o'clock (*M. jalapa*) of flower gardens. Native.

Range Throughout the state.

Habitat Dry soil, roadsides, railways, and disturbed areas.

Blooming Period June–October.

Description Bright red flowers, 1" wide, with 5 petals, slightly toothed or untoothed, growing in a loose cluster. Leaves opposite, rounded at the base. Stem slender, weak. Height: 2–4 ft.

Comments Perennial. The common name refers to the sticky substance on the calyx which traps flies and other small insects. This beautiful wildflower is a potentially threatened species. It must be protected from digging and other forms of destruction for its survival. Native.

Range Central Ohio.

Habitat Prairies, dry open woods, and roadsides.

Blooming Period June–August.

Fire Pink
(Silene virginica)
Pink Family (Caryophillaceae)

Bouncing Bet
(Saponaria officinalis)
Pink Family (Caryophyllaceae)

Deptford Pink
(Dianthus armeria)
Pink Family (Caryophyllaceae)

Description Brilliant red flower, 1½" wide, with 5 narrow petals, each deeply notched. Flowers grow in a loose cluster at top of an erect stalk. Leaves opposite. Stem weak. Height: 1–2 ft.

Comments Perennial. Another common name is Catchfly, which refers to the sticky, elongated calyx, which traps insects. The common name "Pink" refers to the family, not the color. When found in a large colony it presents a spectacular display. Since hummingbirds are attracted to red flowers, they are presumed to be the primary pollinators of these scarlet wildflowers. It is similar to the rare Royal Catchfly (*S. regia*), which has petals that lack deep notches. Native.

Range Scattered throughout the southern half of the state.

Habitat Rich wooded slopes, rocky banks, and hillsides.

Blooming Period May–June.

Description Pink (or white) flowers, 1" wide, with 5 petals, growing in dense clusters. Petals indented at tip. Leaves opposite. Stem smooth and strong. Height: 1–2 ft.

Comments Perennial. Also known as Soapwort because colonial housewives crushed the leaves which produced a lather that was used as a substitute for soap. "Bouncing Bet" is an old nickname for a washerwoman. This wildflower spreads by underground stems and forms large colonies. Introduced from Eurasia.

Range Naturalized throughout the state.

Habitat Roadsides and disturbed areas.

Blooming Period July–September.

Description Small pink flower, ½" wide, with 5 petals, with tiny white spots. Leaves opposite, very narrow, and close to the stem. Stem slender, stiff, and erect. Height: 8–24".

Comments Annual. The common name refers to its former abundance near Deptford, England, a suburb of London. The beauty of this flower can be better appreciated by observing it with a hand lens. Introduced from Europe.

Range Naturalized throughout the state.

Habitat Dry fields, roadsides, and meadows.

Blooming Period May–July.

Wild Columbine
(Aquilegia canadensis)
Buttercup Family (Ranunculaceae)

Meadowsweet
(Spiraea latifolia)
Rose Family (Rosaceae)

Queen-of-the-prairie
(Filipendula rubra)
Rose Family (Rosaceae)

David Dister

Description Distinctive drooping red flowers, 1–2" long, with 5 joined petals. Numerous protruding yellow stamens. Compound leaves divided into 3's. Height: 1–2 ft.

Comments Perennial. The genus name comes from Latin (*aquila*) meaning "eagle," and refers to the resemblance of the flower to the talons of the eagle. Each petal has a long, curved spur extending upward. Spurs contain nectar which attracts hummingbirds and long-tongued insects that are essential for pollination. Bumblebees often pierce the spur and steal nectar without pollinating the flower. The Blue Columbine (*A. caerulea*) is the state flower of Colorado. Native.

Range Throughout the state.

Habitat Rich woods and rocky ledges.

Blooming Period April–July.

Description Pale pink (or white) flowers in spreading clusters. Leaves alternate, oval, toothed. A shrub with slender, smooth, reddish-brown stems. Height: 2–5 ft.

Comments The numerous stamens give the flowers a fuzzy appearance. Often growing in old fields from 10–60 years post-abandonment. The use of selective herbicides to kill trees under powerline rights-of-way allows these and other shrubs to continue spreading and developing into a dense shrub cover which outcompetes invading tree seedlings. The flowers are pollinated by bees. Native.

Range Throughout the state.

Habitat Rocky soil, old fields, moist woodlands, meadows, under powerlines, and other shrub-dominated communities.

Blooming Period June–September.

Description Tiny pink flowers, ⅓" wide, with 5 petals, growing in large, dense clusters. Distinctive leaves large, pinnately compound, with 5–7 leaflets. Stem smooth. Height: 2–8 ft.

Comments Perennial. The leaflets are divided and toothed. Toward the base of the plant, the terminal leaflet can be from 4–8" wide, and divided into 7–9 radiating lobes. This stately plant has escaped from cultivation. The showy flowers make these tall plants stand out like royalty in wet prairie areas. Native.

Range At scattered sites throughout the state.

Habitat Moist prairies and meadows.

Blooming Period June–August.

Swamp Rose
(Rosa palustris)
Rose Family (Rosaceae)

Pasture Rose
(Rosa carolina)
Rose Family (Rosaceae)

Red Clover
(Trifolium pratense)
Pea Family (Fabaceae)

Description Pink flower, 1–2" wide, with 5 petals. Stamens yellow, numerous. Leaves alternate, pinnately compound with 5–7 toothed leaflets. Very narrow stipules at the base of the leafstalk. Stem with hooked thorns. Height: 1–7 ft.

Comments Most wild roses are fragrant. They all provide food and cover for many wild birds and animals. This large rose bush is a plant that "likes to keep its feet wet." Native.

Range Throughout the state.

Habitat Swamps, marshes, lake shores, and other wet areas.

Blooming Period June–August.

Description Solitary pink flower, 1–2" wide. Very narrow stipules. Leaves with 5 leaflets, finely toothed, and dull green. Distinctive slender, straight thorns. Height: 1–3 ft.

Comments A low shrub also known as Wild Rose or Carolina Rose. Sharp prickles scattered along the stems. The fruits are bright red hips, ½" in diameter, which persist well into the winter. Rose hips are edible and are rich in vitamin C. These roses are pollinated by bees and other insects. Another wild rose, the Meadow Rose (*R. blanda*), is the state flower of Iowa. Yet another, the Prairie Rose (*R. setigera*), is the state flower of North Dakota. Native.

Range Throughout the state.

Habitat Dry, sandy or rocky soil, pastures, and open woods.

Blooming Period June–July.

Description Reddish-purple (magenta) round-headed clover, ¾" diameter. Leaves with 3 leaflets form the familiar "clover-leaf." Leaflets marked with a white "V" (chevron). Height: 6–16".

Comments Perennial. Red Clover is pollinated almost entirely by long-tongued bumblebees. As with all members of the Pea Family, it stores nitrogen in its root nodules and is used in crop rotation to improve soil fertility. It is commonly cultivated as hay and a pasture crop; however, it does not have the drought resistance of Alfalfa (*Medicago sativa*). Red Clover is the state flower of Vermont. Introduced from Europe.

Range Naturalized and abundant throughout the state.

Habitat Roadsides, old fields, meadows, and disturbed areas.

Blooming Period May–September.

Alsike Clover
(Trifolium hybridum)
Pea Family (Fabaceae)

Crown-vetch
(Coronilla varia)
Pea Family (Fabaceae)

Hoary Tick-trefoil
(Desmodium canescens)
Pea Family (Fabaceae)

Description Pink (sometimes creamy white) clover-head flower, ½" diameter. Leaves with 3 leaflets form the familiar "clover-leaf." No white "V" on leaflets. Flowers and leaves grow from branching stems. Height: 1–2 ft.

Comments Perennial. Brought to America from Sweden in 1839, this clover has been cultivated for hay, pasture, and to enrich the soil with nitrogen. Once widely planted for agriculture, it is now well established as a wildflower. It is pollinated by bees.

Range Naturalized throughout the state.

Habitat Fields, roadsides, and disturbed areas.

Blooming Period May–October.

Description Pink flowers in a distinctive flower head, 1" wide, growing from the leaf axils. Leaves pinnately compound, with 5–10 pairs of leaflets along a center stalk. Stems creeping: 1–2 ft. long.

Comments Perennial. Crown-vetch is frequently planted along highways for erosion control. As do all members of the Pea Family, it captures gaseous nitrogen from the atmosphere and converts it into a usable form that enriches the soil. Introduced from Europe.

Range Naturalized throughout the state.

Habitat Highway roadsides and dry slopes.

Blooming Period June–August.

Description Pink (or purple) flowers, ½" wide, growing in racemes with horizontal branchlets. Seed pods with 3–6 joints, often on stem at same time as flowers. Compound leaves with 3 leaflets, long, hairy leafstalk. Stem hairy. Height: 2–4 ft.

Comments Perennial. The small, triangular seed pods of this common weed have hooked bristles that enable them to "hitch a ride," and thus be dispersed, by adhering to the fur of animals or the clothing of people. It is one of many "stick-tights" or "beggar-ticks." As a member of the Pea (or Legume) Family, this plant serves to enrich the soil with much-needed nitrogen. Native.

Range Throughout the state.

Habitat Dry fields, open woods, thickets, railways, and dry hillsides.

Blooming Period July–September.

Everlasting Pea
(Lathyrus latifolius)
Pea Family (Fabaceae)

Wild Geranium
(Geranium maculatum)
Geranium Family (Geraniaceae)

Fringed Polygala
(Polygala paucifolia)
Milkwort Family (Polygalaceae)

Donalea Phinney

Description Bright pink (white or purple) flowers, 1" wide, in long-stalked racemes. Flowers odorless. Leaflets in single pairs accompanied by tendrils. Distinctive stems and petioles with flat wings. Stipules lance-shaped.

Comments Perennial. Also known as Wild Pea. Tendrils are modified leaves that curl tightly around rigid objects to assist the plant in climbing and supporting the weak stems. Everlasting Pea has escaped from cultivation. It is a distant relative of Sweet Pea (*L. odoratus*) and Garden Pea (*Pisum sativum*). Introduced from Europe.

Range Scattered throughout the state.

Habitat Roadsides, railways, and disturbed areas.

Blooming Period June–September.

Description Pink (to rose-purple) flowers, 1–1½" wide, with 5 petals. Leaves deeply cleft with 5 lobes. Height: 1–2 ft.

Comments Perennial. Also known as Crane's-bill, which describes the fruit, which is an erect capsule resembling the bird's beak. The genus name comes from the Greek (*geranos*) meaning "crane." The capsule is in 5 parts, each containing a single seed. When mature, it splits lengthwise, throwing seeds forcefully away from the plant. A distant relative, the household geranium (*Pelargonium spp.*) belongs to the same family. Native.

Range Throughout the state.

Habitat Rich moist woods, and floodplains.

Blooming Period April–June.

Description Rose-purple flower, ¾" wide, 2 flaring wings formed from the sepals, and tube formed by the petals, fringed at the end. Flowers grow on top of a cluster of leaves. Leaves alternate, egg-shaped. Stem with scale-like leaves. Height: 3–6".

Comments Perennial. Also known as Gay-wings. It also has small cleistogamous flowers at the base of the stem. This delicate, low-growing plant is one of the most beautiful wildflowers in the state. It is an endangered species. Because of its beauty and scarcity, it must be protected from digging and other forms of destruction if it is to survive. Native.

Range Rare. Found in only a few sites in northern Ohio.

Habitat Rich moist woods, woodland openings, and rocky slopes.

Blooming Period May–June.

Swamp Rose-mallow
(Hibiscus moscheutos)
Mallow Family (Malvaceae)

Purple Loosestrife
(Lythrum salicaria)
Loosestrife Family (Lythraceae)

Fireweed
(Epilobium angustifolium)
Evening-primrose Family (Onagraceae)

Jeanne Willis

Description Large pink flower, 4–6" wide, with 5 petals. Stigma with 5 round lobes. Leaves with long stalks. Height: 5–7 ft.

Comments Perennial. This large, showy flower is very conspicuous at a pond's edge. The filaments of the numerous stamens unite to form a tube around the style. It is related to the cultivated Rose-of-Sharon (*H. syriacus*). Native.

Range Eastern half of the state.

Habitat Marshes, shores of lakes and ponds, and wet ditches.

Blooming Period July–September.

Description Bright reddish-purple flowers, ¾" wide, growing in a dense spike. Leaves opposite, sometimes in whorls of 3, lance-shaped, the lower ones clasping the stem. Height: 2–6 ft.

Comments Perennial. Also known as Spiked Loosestrife. These plants are typical of wetland species in that they expend a considerable amount of energy toward stem growth. They grow in large colonies, often blanketing large areas with their bright color. Each inflorescence can produce up to a phenomenal 300,000 seeds. In addition, the plants can reproduce vegetatively from the roots. This species is very aggressive, becoming abundant in many local areas, and crowding out native cattails and other wetland plants which are valuable to waterfowl and other wildlife. Introduced from Eurasia.

Range Naturalized and locally abundant throughout the state.

Habitat Wetlands, roadside ditches, swamps, and other wet, disturbed areas.

Blooming Period June–September.

Description Purple (to pink) flowers, 1" wide, with 4 petals, growing in a tall raceme. Leaves alternate, lance-shaped, with slightly wavy margins. Stem erect and stout. Height: 3–7 ft.

Comments Perennial. This showy flower is named for the fact that it quickly invades an area that has been burned. Following the May 18, 1980, eruption of Mount St. Helens in Washington, Fireweed was one of the first pioneer plants to invade and establish itself in the blast area. The slender seed pods are about 3" long. They break open to release numerous seeds with white plumes, which are dispersed great distances by the wind. This fast-growing species is pollinated by bees and hummingbirds. Native.

Range Northern counties of the state.

Habitat Open fields, clearings, railways, and roadsides; but most abundant in burned-over areas.

Blooming Period June–August.

Ken Hays

Trailing Arbutus
(*Epigaea repens*)
Heath Family (Ericaceae)

Jeanne Willis

Mountain Laurel
(*Kalmia latifolia*)
Heath Family (Ericaceae)

Description Showy pink (to white) flowers, ¾" wide, growing in a terminal cluster. Flowers cup-shaped, with 10 small pouches projecting from the sides. Leaves alternate, leathery, pointed at both ends. Shrub. Height: 10–20 ft.

Comments E. Lucy Braun described Mountain Laurel as one of America's most beautiful shrubs. As the flowers open, the anthers are caught in the pouches. When an insect touches the flower, the anther springs out, throwing pollen on the insect. The leaves are evergreen. The shrubs often form dense thickets. It is the state flower of Connecticut and Pennsylvania. Native.

Range The unglaciated counties of southeastern Ohio.

Habitat Rocky, sandy acid soil of oak and hemlock woodlands.

Blooming Period May–June.

Description Pink (to white) flowers, ½" wide, growing in terminal clusters. Individual flower is a short tube flaring into 5 lobes. Intensely fragrant. Leaves alternate, thick, and oval-shaped. A trailing plant up to 15 ft. long, growing low to the ground. Height: 2–3".

Comments The leaves are green throughout the year. The flowers have a spicy fragrance. Trailing Arbutus is often found growing in large patches nearly covering the ground. Pollination occurs most commonly by queen bumblebees. This is one of Ohio's earliest showy wildflowers. Native.

Range Eastern half of the state.

Habitat In acid soil of of dry, rocky woods, most particularly in evergreen woodlands.

Blooming Period March–May.

Swamp Milkweed
(*Asclepias incarnata*)
Milkweed Family (Asclepiadaceae)

Rose-pink
(*Sabatia angularis*)
Gentian Family (Gentianaceae)

Scarlet Pimpernel
(*Anagallis arvensis*)
Primrose Family (Primulaceae)

Description Brick-red (to orange) flowers, ¼–½" wide, with 5 petals, growing on long stalks from the axils of the leaves. Leaves opposite, less than 1" long. A low, sprawling plant. Height: 4–12".

Comments Annual. Also known as Poorman's Weatherglass because the flowers close in cloudy or bad weather. It often invades gardens, but seldom is a problem. Introduced from Europe.

Range Naturalized throughout the state.

Habitat Roadsides, fields, lawns, gardens, and disturbed areas.

Blooming Period May–August.

Description Pink flower, 1" wide, with 5 petals. Each flower has a green "eye." Leaves opposite, the base somewhat clasping the stem. Stem 4-angled. Height: 1–3 ft.

Comments Biennial. Also known as Marsh-pink. The species name comes from the Latin (*angulos*) meaning "having sides," in reference to the stem. This is one of the more attractive midsummer wildflowers. It is a highly adaptive plant, growing in a variety of habitats. Native.

Range East-central and southern Ohio.

Habitat Dry to moist fields, pastures, woodland openings, and roadsides.

Blooming Period July–September.

Description Pink flowers in a showy cluster, 1–2½" wide. Distinctive leaves opposite, narrow, lance-shaped, tapering at the tip. Narrow, spindle-shaped seed pods. Stem smooth, with milky juice. Height: 2–4 ft.

Comments Perennial. A wetland milkweed that differs from other milkweeds in having a smooth stem and narrow, lance-shaped leaves. Close examination of individual flowers reveals that the 5 petals resemble a tiny crown. Native.

Range Throughout the state.

Habitat Marshes, swamps, shores, wet ditches, and other moist areas.

Blooming Period July–August.

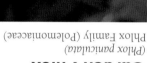

Hound's Tongue
(*Cynoglossum officinale*)
Borage Family (Boraginaceae)

Garden Phlox
(*Phlox paniculata*)
Phlox Family (Polemoniaceae)

Common Milkweed
(*Asclepias syriaca*)
Milkweed Family (Asclepiadaceae)

Description Pink (to lavender) flowers in drooping, round clusters, 2–4" wide. Flowers fragrant. Leaves, large, thick, and softly downy underneath. Height: 3–5 ft.

Comments Perennial. The common name comes from the white, milky sap (*DO NOT EAT*). The Monarch butterfly feeds on the nectar and frequently lays its eggs on the Common Milkweed. The Monarch caterpillars feed on the leaves, which contain glycosides that make the larvae and adult butterflies toxic to, and thus avoided by, predatory birds. The spindle-shaped seedpods have a soft warty surface. In late summer, the pods split open revealing tightly packed seeds with silky "parachutes" that disperse the seeds in the wind. During World War II, the "silk" was used as a substitute for kapok in life jackets. Native.

Range Common throughout the state.

Habitat Riverbanks, roadsides, railways, open fields, and disturbed areas.

Blooming Period June–August.

Description Pink (to lavender or white) flowers, 1" long, with 5 petals, joined to form a tube, growing in a dense, terminal cluster. Style reaching beyond middle of corolla-tube. Leaves opposite, lance-shaped. Stem erect and stout. Height: 3–6 ft.

Comments Perennial. Also known as Fall Phlox because it blooms in the late summer and early autumn. The bright pink flower clusters of these plants offer a striking contrast with the dark green foliage of late summer. It has escaped from gardens and is often found at old homesites. Native.

Range Throughout much of the state.

Habitat Moist woods, thickets, and stream-banks.

Blooming Period July–September.

Description Reddish-purple (to maroon) flowers, ⅓" wide, with 5 lobes. Leaves large, oblong. Stem very leafy, with soft hairs. Height: 1–3 ft.

Comments Perennial. When crushed, the leaves emit a mouse-like odor. The fruits are small nutlets, which are covered with hooked spines that attach to animal fur and human clothing and are thus dispersed. Introduced from Eurasia.

Range Naturalized throughout most of the state; however, absent from many southern and central counties.

Habitat Fields, roadsides, railways, and disturbed areas.

Blooming Period May–June.

Motherwort
(*Leonurus cardiaca*)
Mint Family (Lamiaceae)

Obedient Plant
(*Physostegia virginiana*)
Mint Family (Lamiaceae)

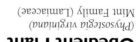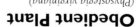

Germander
(*Teucrium canadense*)
Mint Family (Lamiaceae)

Description Pink flowers, ½" long, in a dense spike. Flower forms a single 5-lobed lower lip, open at top, with stamens projecting upwards. Leaves opposite, lance-shaped, toothed, without the fragrance of mint. Stem square and downy. Height: 1–4 ft.

Comments Perennial. Also known as Wood Sage. Look for the distinctive pistil which curves above the flower tube. Native.

Range Throughout the state.

Habitat Marshes, wet ditches, low wet ground, and stream margins.

Blooming Period June–August.

Description Reddish-purple flowers, 1" long, upper lip hooded, lower lip 3-lobed and spotted. They grow in 4 vertical rows on a spike, 4–8" tall. Leaves opposite, lance-shaped, toothed. Stem 4-sided. Height: 1–4 ft.

Comments Perennial. Also known as Obedience and False Dragonhead. The common name refers to the fact that when the spike or individual flowers are pushed to one side, they remain in that position. Native.

Range Throughout the state.

Habitat Swamps, streambanks, wet thickets, and other wet areas.

Blooming Period July–October.

Description Pink (or white) flowers, ½" long, growing in the the leaf axils. Upper lip arched, hairy. Distinctive leaves long-petioled, deeply divided into 3 sharp lobes pointing toward the tip. Stem square. Height: 2–5 ft.

Comments Perennial. This mint requires water but relatively little direct sunlight. The pollination of the flowers is carried out by various bees. It was formerly cultivated as a home-remedy, but is now naturalized as a wild-flower. Introduced from Europe.

Range Throughout the state.

Habitat Woodland borders, thickets, road-sides, and disturbed areas.

Blooming Period June–September.

Henbit
(Lamium amplexicaule)
Mint Family (Lamiaceae)

Oswego Tea
(Monarda didyma)
Mint Family (Lamiaceae)

Wood-betony
(Pedicularis canadensis)
Snapdragon Family (Scrophulariaceae)

Description Reddish-purple flowers, ½–¾" long, with the corolla fused to form a long tube with a hooded upper lip and a flaring lower lip. Upper leaves rounded with scalloped margins, and clasping the square stem. Height: 6–12".

Comments Annual. This is a sprawling plant with stems growing upward from their creeping position. The interesting flowers grow at the top of the stems. Introduced from Eurasia.

Range Naturalized throughout much of the state.

Habitat Roadsides, grassy fields, lawns, cemeteries, and open woodlands.

Blooming Period March–May.

Description Brilliant scarlet flowers in a ragged, round cluster, 2" wide. One terminal flower head to a branch. Leaves opposite, each pair at right angles to the adjacent pair. Stem square, typical of the Mint Family. Height: 2–3 ft.

Comments Perennial. Also known as Bee-balm. The genus is named for Nicholas Monardes (1493–1588) a Spanish botanist who published a book in 1571 with the first picture of a plant from the New World. The leaves have a strong mint odor and flavor. The plant is named for the Oswego Indians who lived along the shore of Lake Ontario in New York and brewed tea from the leaves. The bright red color commonly attracts hummingbirds which pollinate the flowers as they search for nectar. This beautiful, showy wildflower certainly deserves to be protected. Native.

Range Common in northeastern Ohio, and at scattered sites in the west and south.

Habitat Wet, open woodlands, thickets, stream margins, and ditches.

Blooming Period June–August.

Description Red (or yellow) flowers, ¾" long, in a dense, terminal flower cluster. Upper lip arched over 3-lobed lower lip. Leaves alternate, deeply divided lobes, and hairy. Height: 6–18".

Comments Perennial. Also known as Lousewort. The genus name comes from the Latin (*pediculus*) meaning "louse." Ancient farmers had the misconception that cattle became infested with lice when grazing on the plants. It is usually found growing in colonies. Native.

Range Grows throughout much of the state, but absent from most west-central counties.

Habitat Woodland openings and borders.

Blooming Period April–June.

Trumpet-creeper
(Campsis radicans)
Bignonia Family (Bignoniaceae)

Trumpet Honeysuckle
(Lonicera sempervirens)
Honeysuckle Family (Caprifoliaceae)

Cardinal Flower
(Lobelia cardinalis)
Bellflower Family (Campanulaceae)

Description Reddish-orange trumpet-shaped flower, 2½–3" long, in terminal clusters. Leaves opposite, pinnately compound with 7–11 sharply toothed leaflets. Stem woody. A woody vine, climbing or sometimes trailing.

Comments Trumpet Creeper often climbs fenceposts and trees. It climbs with the help of aerial rootlets on its stems. Some people with sensitive skin may develop a dermatitis following contact with the leaves. The bright reddish flowers make it a favorite of hummingbirds. Native.

Range Common throughout southern Ohio, and naturalized at scattered sites northward.

Habitat Moist woods, thickets, and roadsides.

Blooming Period July–September.

Description Scarlet trumpet-shaped flowers, 1–2" long, growing in whorls at the ends of branches. Berries are red. Leaves dark green, opposite, egg-shaped, the upper pairs joined at the stem. Stem woody, smooth; climbing and twining vine.

Comments The genus is named for Adam Lonitzer, a 16th-century German physician and botanist. In their quest for the sweet nectar, hummingbirds carry pollen from flower to flower. Early Native Americans dried and smoked the leaves as a treatment for asthma. They also chewed the leaves and applied them to bee stings to relieve the pain and reduce the swelling. The present use of this showy plant is mostly limited to landscaping and wildlife habitat. Native.

Range At scattered sites mostly in the eastern and southern counties of the state.

Habitat Thickets, roadsides, and woodland borders.

Blooming Period May–July.

Description Brilliant red flower, 1½" long, in a slender spike. Stamens form a tube that extends well beyond the petals. Leaves alternate, lance-shaped, and toothed. Height: 2–5 ft.

Comments Perennial. The Cardinal Flower is one of our most striking wildflowers. The common name is believed to be an allusion to the bright red robes and caps worn by Roman Catholic Cardinals. It is characteristically tall, as are most plants in wet habitats, where there is abundant moisture and light, the two environmental agents most responsible for lush plant growth. These plants are attractive to hummingbirds, which pollinate the flower as they search for nectar. This beautiful streamside wildflower should be protected and not be picked for any reason. Native.

Range Throughout the state.

Habitat Streambanks, swamps, marshes, wet ditches, and other wet areas.

Blooming Period July–September.

Joe-Pye Weed
(Eupatorium fistulosum)
Aster Family (Asteraceae)

Blazing-star
(Liatris spicata)
Aster Family (Asteraceae)

Purple Coneflower
(Echinacea purpurea)
Aster Family (Asteraceae)

Description Pink flowers in rounded clusters. Leaves in whorls of 4's and 5's, bluntly toothed. Stem purple, smooth, hollow. Height: 4–7 ft.

Comments Perennial. According to folklore, Joe Pye was a Native American who used this plant for medicinal purposes. As a wet-habitat species, Joe-Pye Weed spends a considerable amount of energy devoted toward stem growth and numerous flowers. Spicebush Swallowtail butterflies feed on the nectar. Native.

Range Mostly in the unglaciated region of the state.

Habitat Floodplains, stream sides, wet thickets, and meadows.

Blooming Period July–September.

Description Bright pink flowers, growing in dense spikes. Leaves lance-shaped, numerous. Stem smooth. Height: 1–5 ft.

Comments Perennial. Also known as Gay-feather. Blazing-star is unusual in that the flowers bloom from the top of the spike downward. This is one of the most beautiful wildflowers of the prairie. Some species of *Liatris* are grown as ornamental plants. Native.

Range At scattered sites throughout the state.

Habitat Wet prairies and prairie remnants.

Blooming Period July–September.

Description Solitary, reddish-purple flower head, 2–4" wide. Ray flowers 10–20, drooping. Disk bristly, dark colored. Lower leaves long-stalked, tapered, and toothed. Stem stout, covered with fine, stiff hairs. Height: 2–5 ft.

Comments Perennial. The genus name comes from the Greek (*echinos*) meaning "spiny," and refers to the mature, dry cone remaining after the petals have fallen. Cultivated varieties are often planted in flower gardens. The roots grow 6 ft. or more deep in the soil; thus the plant is highly resistant to drought. It is very attractive to butterflies and bees in search of nectar. This is one of the most recognized wildflowers of Ohio's prairie openings. Native.

Range Mostly in the southern half of the state and in other scattered prairie openings.

Habitat Prairies, prairie remnants, dry clearings, and railways.

Blooming Period June–October.

Spotted Knapweed

(Centaurea maculosa)
Aster Family (Asteraceae)

Description Pink (to purple) thistle-like heads, ¾" wide. A highly branched plant. Bracts with black tips. Leaves deeply cleft into narrow segments. Stem smooth. Height: 1–3 ft.

Comments Biennial. Also known as Star-thistle. The common name refers to the spotted appearance created by the black-tipped bracts beneath the flower heads. Knapweeds have escaped from cultivation and are now established as wildflowers. Introduced from Europe.

Range At scattered sites throughout the state.

Habitat Roadsides and disturbed areas.

Blooming Period June–October.

Blue and Purple Flowers

Asiatic Dayflower
(Commelina communis)
Spiderwort Family (Commelinaceae)

Ohio Spiderwort
(Tradescantia ohiensis)
Spiderwort Family (Commelinaceae)

Pickerelweed
(Pontederia cordata)
Pickerelweed Family (Pontederiaceae)

David Dister

Description Bright, sky-blue flower, ½" wide, with 2 blue petals above and 1 distinctive, small white petal below. Leaves with bases forming a sheath around the stem. Stem weak and reclining. Height: 6–15".

Comments Annual. Resembles Virginia Dayflower (*C. virginica*), a native perennial with more erect growth habit and all three petals blue. The common name refers to the fact that each flower blooms for only a single day. The genus is named for 3 early Dutch botanists, referred to by Linnaeus in *Critica botanica*. Two of them, Jan (1629–1692) and his brother's son, Caspar II (1667–1731)—represented by the blue petals—made significant contributions to botany. In the third generation, Caspar III (1700–1734)—represented by the white petal—died at an early age before he was able to accomplish much. Introduced from Asia.

Range Naturalized throughout Ohio.

Habitat Moist, shaded places, streambanks, and roadsides.

Blooming Period June–October.

Description Bright blue (to purple) flower, 1½" wide, with 3 petals, growing in a terminal cluster. Stamens 6, yellow, with distinctively hairy filaments. Flower stalks and bracts smooth. Leaves long, narrow, and pointed. Height: 1–3 ft.

Comments Perennial. The common name refers to the spider-like appearance of the 2 long, leaf-like bracts beneath the flowers. The term "wort" is an old English word meaning "plant." The genus is named in honor of John Tradescant (1608–1662) who was the botanist and gardener to King Charles I of Great Britain (1625–1649). The plant is pollinated by bumblebees, which eat the pollen. The transparent hairs of the filaments of Spiderworts have long been a favorite specimen of biology students for observing the flowing cytoplasm and nucleus of living cells under a microscope. Native.

Range Throughout the state.

Habitat Railways, roadsides, wet thickets, and wet meadows.

Blooming Period May–July.

Description Blue flowers in a spike, 3–4" tall. Distinctive leaves basal, arrowhead-shaped, 4–10" long. Height: 1–4 ft.

Comments Perennial. The common name refers to the plant growing in water in which the fish, pickerel, are likely to be found. The species name comes from the Latin (*cord* and *atus*) meaning "heart-shaped," in reference to the heart-shaped leaves. This plant is characterized as an emerging aquatic plant with stout petioles supporting the leaves high above the water. The seeds are eaten by deer, and muskrats feed on the rootstocks. Native.

Range Most frequent in the northern part of the state, and at scattered sites elsewhere.

Habitat Swamps, shallow pond water, and marshes.

Blooming Period June–October.

Cindy Tucci

Crested Dwarf Iris
(Iris cristata)
Iris Family (Iridaceae)

Jeanne Willis

Blue-eyed Grass
(Sisyrinchium angustifolium)
Iris Family (Iridaceae)

Ken Hays

Wild Hyacinth
(Camassia scilloides)
Lily Family (Liliaceae)

Description Pale blue flowers, ¾" wide, with 6 petals, growing in a raceme. Linear leaves are keeled. Height: 1–2 ft.

Comments Perennial. Also known as Camass. The genus name is derived from the Native American (*quamash*). The bulbs were commonly used for food by Native Americans and early explorers. The Easter Hyacinth (*Hyacinthus orientalis*) is a Eurasian species. Native.

Range Throughout much of the state.

Habitat Open and shaded floodplain woods and along streams. In the southwestern counties, the usual habitat is steep, rocky, calcareous wooded slopes. In the Lake Erie Islands, it is common in the "hackberry woods."

Blooming Period May–June.

Description Blue flower, ½" wide, with 6 petals, each with a small point at the tip. Flower on a long stalk. Leaves stiff, narrow, and grasslike. Stem flat. Height: 6–24".

Comments Perennial. Not a true grass, but owes its common name to its winged stem and grasslike leaves. The thin stem and leaves are deceiving because from its underground bulb grows an erect and stiff plant which sways but never breaks under the wind. The two edges of the stem reinforce the stem, a principle used by engineers when designing beams that span long distances. Following pollination by bees and flies, the flowers develop seeds in brown capsules. Native.

Range Throughout the state.

Habitat Roadsides, wet meadows, pastures, and open woods.

Blooming Period May–July.

Description Solitary, blue flower, 2" wide, with 3 petals and 3 bearded sepals. Leaves lance-shaped, forming a sheath around the stem. Height: 3–8".

Comments Perennial. The common name refers to the down-curved sepals with a distinctive yellow crest. This iris often grows in large patches from rhizomes that are highly branched and close to the surface of the ground, with the roots growing downward from the bottom. They grow best in light shade and well-drained soil. Native.

Range Northeastern and southern counties of the state.

Habitat Acid soil of rich woods, wooded hillsides, and ravines.

Blooming Period April–May.

Ken Hays

Dwarf Larkspur
(Delphinium tricorne)
Buttercup Family (Ranunculaceae)

Sharp-lobed Hepatica
(Hepatica acutiloba)
Buttercup Family (Ranunculaceae)

Dwarf Iris
(Iris verna)
Iris Family (Iridaceae)

Description Blue flowers, 2–3" wide, with 3 petals and 3 down-curved sepals with wide yellow bands, slightly hairy, but without a crest. Very fragrant. Leaves narrow, erect, bright green, ½" wide and 12" tall. Flower stalk 4–6" tall.

Comments Perennial. The genus is named for Iris, the mythological Greek goddess of the rainbow. Although not a lily, a European variety of Iris served as the model for the *fleur-de-lis*, the coat of arms of the former royal family of France. In their search for nectar, insects must force their way under the style branch, past the stamens and stigma, thus pollinating the flower. This plant is related to the cultivated, commercial Garden Iris (*I. germanica*), sometimes also known as "flags." This rare plant is a threatened species and must be protected. Native.

Range Limited areas in southern Ohio.

Habitat Dry sandy, acid soil, oak woods, and pine woods.

Blooming Period April–May.

Description Blue (pink or white) flowers, 1" wide, with 6–12 petal-like sepals. Stamens numerous. Three green sepal-like bracts beneath the flower. Distinctive leaves with 3 deep lobes, pointed at the tips. Stem very hairy. Height: 4–6".

Comments Perennial. The genus name comes from the Greek (*hepar*) meaning "liver," in reference to the shape of the leaf, resembling the 3 lobes of a mammal's liver. In early times, according to the Doctrine of Signatures, people believed that a plant's appearance provided a clue to its medicinal use. It was thought that extracts from the leaves of Hepatica could be used to treat liver ailments. However, there is no scientific basis for this use. It is one of Ohio's earliest spring wildflowers. It is similar to Round-lobed Hepatica (*H. americana*), which has leaves with rounded tips. Native.

Range Throughout the state.

Habitat Rich woods with calcareous soil.

Blooming Period March–May.

Description Blue (to purple) flowers, 1½" long, growing in a raceme. Sepals 5, petal-like. Upper sepal forms a long spur. Leaves deeply divided, mostly at base of plant. Height: 1–2 ft.

Comments Perennial. Due to their bright color, the 5 sepals are often mistaken for petals. There are 4 tiny petals, the upper 2 actually enclosed within the spur. The flower bears little resemblance to a buttercup; however, the stamens are numerous, which is a characteristic of the Buttercup Family. Larkspurs contain an alkaloid that is poisonous to cattle. Native.

Range Scattered throughout the state.

Habitat In calcareous soils of rich woods.

Blooming Period April–May.

Northern Monkshood
(Aconitum noveboracense)
Buttercup Family (Ranunculaceae)

Dame's Rocket
(Hesperis matronalis)
Mustard Family (Brassicaceae)

Purple Cress
(Cardamine douglassii)
Mustard Family (Brassicaceae)

Cindy Tucci

Description Blue (or violet) flowers, ¾" long, growing in short clusters. Distinctive upper sepal helmet-shaped, covers 2 petals. Leaves deeply cleft into 3–5 segments. Stem hairy. Height: 2–3 ft.

Comments Perennial. This unique flower presents the image of a hooded monk. The plant grows from a tuber which contains aconine, an alkaloid that is especially poisonous to mammals. However, as a very rare wildflower, it is an endangered species and must be protected for its survival. Native.

Range Rare. Only at a few sites in northeastern Ohio.

Habitat Moist sandstone cliffs, cool shaded ravines, and streambanks.

Blooming Period July–August.

Description Purple (pink or white) flowers, ¾–1" wide, with 4 petals, growing in terminal racemes. Long, upward pointing seedpods, characteristic of the mustard family. Flowers very fragrant. Leaves alternate, long, pointed, and toothed. Stems hairy. Height: 2–3 ft.

Comments Biennial. The common name "rocket" is a European name given to any plant in the genus *Hesperis*. "Dame" is a term used in reference to a matronly woman. The species name comes from the Latin (*matrona*) meaning a woman who has an established social position. Such a woman would certainly stand tall. This is an old-fashioned garden plant that has escaped from cultivation and now is widespread as a wildflower. It may be confused with Garden Phlox (*Phlox paniculata*), which has 5 petals and blooms much later in the season. Introduced from Eurasia.

Range Naturalized throughout Ohio.

Habitat Moist, shady places, fields, roadsides, and old homesteads.

Blooming Period May–June.

Description Pale purple (to pale pink) flowers, ½–¾," with 4 petals. Stem leaves alternate. Basal leaves round with long petioles and purple undersides. Stem hairy. Height: 6–12".

Comments Perennial. The 4 petals form a cross, which is a characteristic of the Mustard Family. The alternative name of that family is Cruciferae, which comes from the Latin (*cruci*) meaning a cross. It is similar to Spring Cress (*C. rhomboidea*), which has white petals and smooth stems. Native.

Range Throughout the state.

Habitat Rich, moist woods and floodplains.

Blooming Period March–May.

Common Blue Violet
(Viola sororia)
Violet Family (Violaceae)

Purple Milkwort
(Polygala sanguinea)
Milkwort Family (Polygalaceae)

Hairy Vetch
(Vicia villosa)
Pea Family (Fabaceae)

Description Purple flowers, ¾" long, with petals having white tips, on a long-stalked, 1-sided raceme with more than 10 flowers. Compound leaves with 6–8 pairs of thin leaflets and terminating with curling, twisting tendrils. Stem with distinctive spreading hairs. Height: 2–3 ft.

Comments Annual. Vetches are showy and colorful, and are thus pollinated by insects, mostly bees. This plant is commonly planted for hay and as a winter cover crop in cultivated fields. Vetches are in the Pea Family, and share a common ability to transform nitrogen from the air for the benefit of the plant and the enrichment of the soil after the plant dies. It has escaped from cultivation. It is similar to Cow Vetch (*V. cracca*), which has a smooth stem. Introduced from Eurasia.

Range Naturalized throughout the state.

Habitat Fields, fencerows, roadsides, and thickets.

Blooming Period May–August.

Description Rose-purple dense flower heads, ½" thick, growing at the ends of the branches. Leaves alternate. Height: 6–15".

Comments Annual. Also known as Field Milkwort or Blood Milkwort. The species name comes from the Latin (*sanguin*) meaning "blood," in reference to the color of the flower, resembling that of venous blood. It reproduces only by seed. Native.

Range Absent from west and some central counties, otherwise throughout the state.

Habitat Fields, meadows, and roadsides.

Blooming Period June–September.

Description Blue (to deep purple) flower, 1" wide, with 5 petals, the lower petal spurred. Smooth stalk. Flowers and leaves on separate stalks. Leaves heart-shaped. Height: 3–8".

Comments Perennial. Violets have several reproductive strategies that greatly enhance their chances of survival in competitive environments. In addition to the formation of seeds, Blue Violets grow in large clumps formed by spreading horizontal stems (rhizomes), which grow close to the surface of the ground. In the summer, they form cleistogamous flowers that do not open, but self-pollinate within the enclosed calyx. The leaves are rich in vitamins A and C and can be used in salads or cooked as greens. It is the state flower of Wisconsin, Illinois, Rhode Island, and New Jersey. Native.

Range Common and locally abundant throughout the state.

Habitat Wooded floodplains and slopes, moist open woods and fields, lawns and other disturbed grassy sites.

Blooming Period March–June.

Fringed Gentian
(*Gentianopsis crinita*)
Gentian Family (Gentianaceae)

Periwinkle
(*Vinca minor*)
Dogbane Family (Apocynaceae)

Common Morning-glory
(*Ipomoea purpurea*)
Morning-glory Family (Convolvulaceae)

George Phinney

Description Bright blue tubular flower, 2" long, with 4 delicately fringed petals, at the tips of terminal branches. Leaves opposite, rounded base, pointed tip. Stem erect and slender. Height: 1–3 ft.

Comments Annual. This beautiful species is one of the last wildflowers to bloom in late summer and early fall. The flowers are open only in sunshine and close tightly in the shade. Reproduction is by seeds only. The seeds do not survive drying. Extensive collection of the flowers easily leads to the plant's extinction. It is an endangered species and must not be picked. Native.

Range Northern counties and at a few scattered sites elsewhere in the state.

Habitat Wet eroding calcareous slopes, wet woodland openings, meadows and marshy areas.

Blooming Period September–October.

Description Solitary blue flower, 1," with 5 petals. Leaves opposite, dark green, and glossy. A creeping ground cover. Height: 4–6".

Comments Perennial. Also known as Myrtle. It is widely cultivated as a border plant or ground cover throughout much of Ohio. It has escaped from cultivation. Introduced from Europe.

Range Naturalized, mostly in eastern and southern counties.

Habitat Roadsides, railways, cemeteries, open woodlands, old homesites, and other disturbed areas.

Blooming Period March–June.

Description Purple (blue, pink, or white) flower with funnel-shaped corolla 2–3" long. Sepals narrow, pointed. Distinctive broad, heart-shaped leaves. Stem hairy, a twining vine: 10 ft. long.

Comments Annual. The flowers bloom in the morning and close around noon. An old-fashioned garden flower which has escaped from cultivation and is now established as a wildflower. Many people, however, consider Morning-glories to be serious weeds of cultivated fields. Introduced from tropical America.

Range Naturalized over much of the state.

Habitat Moist fields, roadsides, and disturbed areas.

Blooming Period July–November.

Jacob's Ladder
(Polemonium reptans)
Phlox Family (Polemoniaceae)

Wild Blue Phlox
(Phlox divaricata)
Phlox Family (Polemoniaceae)

Miami-mist
(Phacelia purshii)
Waterleaf Family (Hydrophyllaceae)

Jeanne Willis

Description Blue flowers, bell-shaped, ½" wide, in terminal clusters. Stamens not protruding beyond corolla. Leaves pinnately compound, with 7–17 leaflets, that resemble a ladder. Erect stem. Height: 8–15".

Comments Perennial. Also known as Greek Valerian. The white stamens and the blue petals are suggestive of the colors of the Greek flag. Native.

Range Throughout Ohio.

Habitat Moist woods, and wooded floodplains.

Blooming Period April–June.

Description Blue flower, 1" wide, with 5 petals joined together to form a tube. Flowers grow in a loose cluster (raceme) at the top of the stem. Leaves opposite and widely spaced on the stem. Stem sticky and slightly hairy. Height: 10–20".

Comments Perennial. Also known as Wild Sweet William. The flowers are noted for their color, beauty, and fragrance. Native.

Range Throughout Ohio.

Habitat Rich woods, borders, openings, and fields.

Blooming Period April–June.

Description Blue flower, white center, ½" wide, with 5 fringed lobes. Leaves alternate, sharp toothed. Upper leaves are sessile. Lower leaves with long stalks. Height: 6–20".

Comments Annual. We see in a flower a thing of beauty. However, their most important function is to produce seeds which will perpetuate the species. The beauty of this attractive wildflower can be appreciated even more with the use of a hand lens. Native.

Range Throughout the state, but absent in the extreme northwestern counties.

Habitat Floodplains, rich moist woods, and wet meadows.

Blooming Period April–June.

Forget-me-not
(Myosotis scorpioides)
Borage Family (Boraginaceae)

Virginia Bluebells
(Mertensia virginica)
Borage Family (Boraginaceae)

Blue Vervain
(Verbena hastata)
Vervain Family (Verbenaceae)

Description Sky blue flower with a yellow eye, ¼" wide, growing on diverging branches. The corolla is tube-shaped and flares into 5 lobes. Leaves alternate, sessile, and hairy. Stem hairy, sprawling. Height: 6–24".

Comments Perennial. The species name refers to the tightly coiled flower buds which somewhat resemble a scorpion's "tail." Most introduced plants favor roadsides and disturbed areas, but in contrast, Forget-me-not grows in wet areas. It is related to the cultivated species, *M. sylvatica*. Introduced from Europe.

Range Naturalized in the northeastern counties and at scattered sites in other parts of the state.

Habitat Stream and lake shores, swamps, marshes, wet ditches, and other wet areas.

Blooming Period May–October.

Description Blue flowers, 1" long, with nodding, bell-shaped flowers hanging in clusters from the top of the stem. Pink buds open into the light blue flowers. Leaves alternate, smooth, pale blue-green, oval-shaped. Height: 1–2 ft.

Comments Perennial. The genus of this showy spring wildflower is named for Franz Karl Mertens (1764–1831), an early German botanist. With its short blooming season this is one of the many plants known as spring ephemerals. A forest floor carpeted with Virginia Bluebells in early spring will show no traces of the plant by summer. Native.

Range Throughout much of the state, but absent from most northwestern counties.

Habitat Rich woods and moist floodplains.

Blooming Period April–May.

Description Blue (to violet) flowers in branching, tall, thin spikes. The spikes have only a few flowers open at a time, starting at the base and proceeding upwards. Leaves lance-shaped, toothed. Height: 2–6 ft.

Comments Perennial. The genus name comes from the Latin (*verbena*) meaning "holy plant." The plant is pollinated by bumblebees. Through the winter, the dead tops of the plants persist, providing food for many birds. Native.

Range Throughout the state.

Habitat Wet fields, lake and stream borders, ditches, and other wet disturbed areas.

Blooming Period July–September.

Showy Skullcap
(Scutellaria serrata)
Mint Family (Lamiaceae)

Ground-ivy
(Glechoma hederacea)
Mint Family (Lamiaceae)

Self-heal
(Prunella vulgaris)
Mint Family (Lamiaceae)

Description Blue flowers, 1" long, growing in a raceme. Leaves opposite, stalked, distinctive toothed margins. Stem square, smooth. Height: 1–2 ft.

Comments Perennial. The common name refers to the tubed flower with 2 lips. The upper lip is hooded, looking much like a tight-fitting cap. The species name comes from the Latin (*serra*) meaning "saw," referring to the saw-toothed margins of the leaves. This plant is a potentially threatened species and must be protected for its survival. Native.

Range South-central counties of the state.
Habitat Rich woods and roadside banks.
Blooming Period May–June.

Description Blue flowers, ½" long, in whorls in the leaf axils. A creeping ivy-like plant. Leaves long-stalked and bluntly toothed. Stem square. Height: 6–8".

Comments Perennial. Also known as Gill-over-the-ground. Though Ground-ivy may be regarded by some people as a problem in lawns and gardens, it makes an attractive ground cover. When crushed, the leaves have a distinctive pungent odor. Introduced from Eurasia.

Range Naturalized throughout the state.
Habitat Open woods, fields, roadsides, lawns, and other disturbed areas.
Blooming Period March–July.

Description Purple flowers, ½" long, in a dense, terminal, flat-topped spike. Individual flower has a hoodlike upper lip. Flowers mixed with sharp-pointed bracts. Only a few flowers are open at one time. As with other mints, it has opposite leaves and square stems. Height: 3–12".

Comments Perennial. Also known as Heal-all because it is presumed to have been introduced by early settlers for a variety of medicinal purposes. It has an unusually long blooming period. Introduced from Eurasia.

Range Naturalized throughout the state.
Habitat Roadsides, fields, lawns, and other disturbed areas.
Blooming Period May–October.

Purple Dead-nettle

(Lamium purpureum)
Mint Family (Lamiaceae)

Purple Bergamot

(Monarda media)
Mint Family (Lamiaceae)

Wild Bergamot

(Monarda fistulosa)
Mint Family (Lamiaceae)

Description Purple flowers, ½–¾" long, corolla fused to form a long tube with a hooded upper lip and a flaring lower lip. Leaves opposite. Upper leaves short-stemmed. Lower leaves long-stemmed. Stem square. Height: 6–12".

Comments Annual. The opposite leaves and square stem make this plant easy to recognize as a member of the Mint Family. This plant is generally considered to be a weed. It is similar to Spotted Dead-nettle (*L. maculatum*), which has a broad white stripe along the midvein. Introduced from Eurasia.

Range Naturalized throughout the state.

Habitat Roadsides, cultivated fields, lawns, cemeteries, and disturbed areas.

Blooming Period March–May.

Description Reddish-purple flowers growing in a dense head, 1½" wide. Upper lip without soft, long hairs at the tip. Bracts dark purple. Leaves opposite, stalked. Stem square. Height: 2–3 ft.

Comments Perennial. This attractive member of the Mint Family is generally considered to be a hybrid of Oswego Tea (*M. didyma*) x Wild Bergamot (*M. fistulosa*). Native.

Range Northeastern and south-central counties, and at scattered sites elsewhere.

Habitat Moist woods, thickets, fields, railways, and roadsides.

Blooming Period July–August.

Description Dense, rounded cluster of lavender flowers, 1" long. Individual flowers are slender tubes, each with a distinctive lip. Bracts tinged with purple. Leaves opposite, coarsely toothed. Stem square. Height: 2–4 ft.

Comments Perennial. Also known as Horse-mint. The leaves are aromatic and can be used to make mint tea. It is pollinated by hummingbird moths and bumblebees. Native.

Range Throughout the state.

Habitat In calcareous soils of dry fields, thickets, woodland borders.

Blooming Period July–August.

Downy Wood-mint
(Blephilia ciliata)
Mint Family (Lamiaceae)

Bittersweet Nightshade
(Solanum dulcamara)
Nightshade Family (Solanaceae)

Blue-eyed Mary
(Collinsia verna)
Snapdragon Family (Scrophulariaceae)

Description Purple flowers, with purple bracts growing in whorls at the top of the stem. Leaves opposite, sessile. Stem square, downy. Height: 1–3 ft.

Comments Perennial. The species name comes from the Latin (*cilia*) meaning "hairs" in reference to the fine hairs on the stem. This delicate mint is distinguished by its erect upper lip and spreading lower lip with 3 lobes. Native.

Range Mostly in the eastern and southern counties of the state.

Habitat Woodland openings, borders, thickets, fields, and roadsides.

Blooming Period June–July.

Description Purple flower, ½" wide, with 5 petals swept back. Yellow anthers form a protruding beak. Fruit: green berries that turn bright red at maturity. Leaves with 2 small, distinctive lobes at base. Stem climbing, somewhat woody. Height: 2–8 ft.

Comments Perennial. Also known as Deadly Nightshade. *The berries are poisonous. DO NOT EAT.* Although many species of nightshades are poisonous when eaten, some of our most important plants are members of this family. They include potato, tomato, and tobacco. Introduced from Europe.

Range Naturalized throughout the state.

Habitat Moist thickets and waste places.

Blooming Period May–September.

Description A bicolored flower with blue lower lip and white upper lip, ¾" long, in clusters of loose whorls of 4–6 blossoms. Center lobe of lower lip folded over the stamens, thus giving the appearance of 4 lobes. Leaves opposite. Height: 6–24".

Comments Annual. The genus of this beautiful spring wildflower is named for Zaccheus Collins (1764–1831), an American botanist and vice president of the Philadelphia Academy of Science. The species name comes from the Latin (*vernal*) meaning "of spring." Blue-eyed Mary grows in small patches from seeds dropped the previous year. Often the seeds germinate in the fall, then the plant grows to maturity the next spring. Native.

Range Mostly in the southern counties, and at scattered sites northwards.

Habitat Low, rich woods, wooded floodplains, and open streamsides.

Blooming Period April–June.

Smooth Ruellia
(Ruellia strepens)
Acanthus Family (Acanthaceae)

Jeanne Willis

Sharp-winged Monkey Flower
(Mimulus alatus)
Snapdragon Family (Scrophulariaceae)

Cindy Tucci

Hairy Beardtongue
(Penstemon hirsutus)
Snapdragon Family (Scrophulariaceae)

Description Pale purple flowers, 1" long, with white lips, growing in clusters at the top of the stem. Leaves opposite. Stem hairy. Height: 1–3 ft.

Comments Perennial. The species name comes from the Latin (*hirsutus*) meaning "shaggy" in reference to the hairy stem. With a hand lens, examine the throat of the flower and discover the 4 fertile stamens and 1 sterile stamen, which is densely bearded. Native.

Range Throughout most of the state.

Habitat Dry woodlands, fields, and roadside banks.

Blooming Period May–July.

Description Bluish-purple flower, 1" long, on a short stalk (or sessile). Upper lip 2-lobed; lower lip 3-lobed. Flowers grow in pairs on the stem. Leaves opposite, stalked. Square stem with wings. Height: 1–3 ft.

Comments Perennial. With a little imagination, the flower has a slight resemblance to a monkey's face; thus the genus name *Mimulus* which comes from the Latin (*mimicus*), meaning to mimic or imitate. Similar to the Common Monkey Flower (*M. ringens*), which has long-stalked flowers and stems without wings. Native.

Range Eastern, central, and southern Ohio. Absent from most of the northwestern quarter of the state.

Habitat Streambanks, swamps, and other wet places.

Blooming Period June–September.

Description Bluish-purple trumpet-shaped flower, 2" long, with 5 flaring lobes. 2 small leaves at base of each flower. Stem smooth, square. Height: 1–3 ft.

Comments Perennial. The Ruellias are also known as Wild Petunias. However, the garden variety of petunias are in the genus *Petunia* and are in the Nightshade Family (Solanaceae). The flowers grow either singly or in clusters in the leaf axils. The corolla is radially symmetrical, with 5 equal-sized lobes. Similar to Hairy Ruellia (*R. caroliniensis*), which has hairy stem and leaves. Native.

Range Throughout southern and western Ohio.

Habitat Woodland openings and borders, cliffs, roadsides, and thickets.

Blooming Period May–August.

Lopseed
(Phryma leptostachya)
Lopseed Family (Phrymaceae)

Bluets
(Houstonia caerulea)
Madder Family (Rubiaceae)

Teasel
(Dipsacus sylvestris)
Teasel Family (Dipsacaceae)

Description Small pale purple (or white) flowers, ¼" long, in pairs on a very narrow spike. Corolla 2-lipped, the lower lip longer. Flowers are borne in opposite pairs, each at right angles to the stem when in full bloom. The mature fruit bends down ("lops") against the stem. Leaves opposite, toothed. Height: 1–3 ft.

Comments Perennial. The Lopseed Family has only a single genus and species. The plant will have flowers and fruit on the stem at the same time. The plant is sometimes grown in gardens for its botanical interest rather than its beauty. Native.

Range Throughout Ohio.

Habitat Rich, moist woods and thickets.

Blooming Period July–August.

Description Solitary pale blue flowers, ½" wide, with 4 petals and yellow "eye" in the center. Leaves on stem opposite and small. Basal leaves form a rosette. Stem erect, thin. Height: 2–8".

Comments Perennial. Also known as Quaker Ladies. The genus is named for William Houston (1695–1733), an English botanist. These delicate flowers often grow in large colonies. Pollination is usually carried out by bees and smaller butterflies. What this plant lacks in size is made up for by its beauty. Native.

Range Mostly in the eastern and southern counties of the state.

Habitat Grassy fields, woodland borders, roadsides, and areas of poor soil.

Blooming Period April–June.

Description Pale purple flowers, in a thistle-like head, 1–2" tall. Flowers open starting in a belt around the center of the spike, with new ones open daily in both directions, forming 2 bands of flowers. Leaves opposite, embrace the stem, where they often hold rainwater. Stem prickly. Height: 2–6 ft.

Comments Biennial. The genus name comes from the Greek (*dipsa*) meaning thirst. The plant was given this name because shepherds drank from the water collected in the cup formed by the base of the leaves. Although a very prickly plant, Teasel is not a thistle. The dried flower heads persist on dead stems throughout winter. They are often collected for ornamental arrangements of dried plant materials. Early settlers used the dried flower heads to card wool in preparation for spinning. Introduced from Europe.

Range Naturalized throughout the state.

Habitat Roadsides, fields, railways, and other disturbed open areas.

Blooming Period July–October.

Great Lobelia
(Lobelia siphilitica)
Bellflower Family (Campanulaceae)

Tall Bellflower
(Campanula americana)
Bellflower Family (Campanulaceae)

Venus' Looking-glass
(Triodanis perfoliata)
Bellflower Family (Campanulaceae)

Description Blue (to purple) flowers, ¾" wide, with 5 petals, growing in upper leaf axils. Leaves heart-shaped, clasping the stem. Stem erect. Height: 6–30".

Comments Annual. Venus was the Roman goddess of beauty and love. Perhaps that is what people see when admiring these beautiful blue flowers growing upward from heart-shaped leaves. Native.

Range Mostly in the eastern and southern counties of the state.

Habitat Woodland borders, thickets, railways, and disturbed open areas.

Blooming Period May–July.

Description Blue flowers, 1" wide, with 5 petals, growing in a terminal, leafy spike. Flower shaped more like a star than a bell. Distinctive style is curved downward, then up at the tip. Height: 2–6 ft.

Comments Biennial. This attractive blue flower matches the summer sky. Children often remark that the style is curved like an elephant's trunk. The stamens curve outwards thus assuring that the pollen-laden anthers are distant enough so there is little chance of pollen falling on the stigma resulting in self-fertilization. Cross-fertilization is necessary in order to ensure a healthy, vigorous species. The flowers are pollinated by honeybees and yellowjackets. Native.

Range Throughout the state.

Habitat Rich, moist thickets, woods, and roadsides.

Blooming Period June–September.

Description Bright blue flowers, 1" long, 2-lipped, the lower lip striped with white. Flowers in leaf axils in an elongated cluster on a leafy stem. Leaves alternate, slightly toothed, with pointed tip. Height: 1–3 ft.

Comments Perennial. It is easy to see how pollination occurs as a bee covered with pollen is forced to brush the hooked-shaped stigma as it crawls in and out of the flower tube. The species name, *siphilitica,* is based on the plant providing a substance that Native Americans believed to be a cure for syphilis. A showy wildflower of late summer and early autumn. Native.

Range Throughout the state.

Habitat Low damp ground, streambanks, wet woods, and wet roadside ditches.

Blooming Period July–October.

Tall Ironweed
(*Vernonia gigantea*)
Aster Family (Asteraceae)

Spiked Lobelia
(*Lobelia spicata*)
Bellflower Family (Campanulaceae)

Downy Lobelia
(*Lobelia puberula*)
Bellflower Family (Campanulaceae)

Description Blue flowers, ¾" long, tube-shaped with white throat, flaring into 5 distinctive lobes. Flowers grow in a distinctive 1-sided tall spike. Leaves alternate, toothed, downy. Stem downy. Height: 1–3 ft.

Comments Perennial. The genus is named for Mathias de Lobel (1538–1616) the Flemish botanist who taught the value of leaves in plant classification. His book *Kruydtboeck* (1581) contained many excellent wood engravings. The species name comes from the Latin (*pubescens*) meaning hairy or downy. Close examination reveals 2 upper lobes and 3 lower lobes. This attractive flower of the late summer favors growing in dry areas. It is similar to Great Lobelia (*L. siphilitica*), which has flowers growing on all sides of the spike. Native.

Range Southern counties of the state.

Habitat Woodland borders, clearings, and roadsides.

Blooming Period July–October.

Description Pale blue (to white) flowers, ½" long, growing in a loose-clustered spike. Leaves alternate, lance-shaped, stalkless. Height: 1–3 ft.

Comments Perennial. The flowers are typical of the lobelias, having a bilaterally symmetric, tubular corolla. The upper lip has 2 lobes, while the lower lip has 3 lobes. Native.

Range Mostly in the eastern half of the state, generally absent from the west-central counties.

Habitat Dry woods, woodland borders, railways, and roadsides.

Blooming Period June–August.

Description Deep purple (to magenta) flowers, ¾" wide, growing in dense clusters. Bracts surrounding flower heads are blunt-tipped. Leaves alternate, lance-shaped, finely toothed. Branches spreading. Stems purple, with very short hairs. Height: 3–10 ft.

Comments Perennial. The common name is very descriptive of the height and the strong stem. Ironweed grows tallest in rich, moist soils; it grows shorter in drier soils. This stately plant is very conspicuous in the fields of summer. Many species of butterflies are attracted to the flowers. Native.

Range Common and widely distributed throughout the state.

Habitat Moist fields, thickets, and roadsides.

Blooming Period August–October.

Mist-flower
(Eupatorium coelestinum)
Aster Family (Asteraceae)

Arrow-leaved Aster
(Aster sagittifolius)
Aster Family (Asteraceae)

New England Aster
(Aster novae-angliae)
Aster Family (Asteraceae)

Description Blue (to purple) flowers, with 30–40 per head, in flat-topped clusters (umbels). Leaves opposite, stalked, toothed. Stem slightly downy. Height: 1–3 ft.

Comments Perennial. These attractive blue flowers usually turn purple as they age. The individual flowers have blue disk flowers but no ray flowers. Due to its resemblance to the garden ageratum (*Ageratum houstonianum*) Mist-flower has been cultivated under the name of Hardy Ageratum. Native.

Range Mostly in the southern counties of the state.

Habitat Woodland borders, thickets, streambanks, and field margins.

Blooming Period July–October.

Description Pale blue flower head, ⅝" wide, with purple disk. Bracts of flower heads narrow, with a central green stripe. Leaves narrow, arrowhead-shaped, toothed, with winged stalks. Stem smooth. Height: 2–5 ft.

Comments Perennial. The species name comes from the Latin (*sagitta* and *folia*) meaning "arrow-leaved" in reference to the shape of the leaves. Likewise, Sagittarius is the constellation known as the Archer. Native.

Range Widely distributed throughout the state.

Habitat Streambanks and woodlands.
Blooming Period August–October.

Description Bright purple flower head, 1–2" wide, with 40–50 rays. Disk yellow. Numerous flower heads clustered at the top of the plant. Leaves lance-shaped, toothless, clasping the stem. Stem stout, hairy. Height: 2–8 ft.

Comments Perennial. The genus name comes from the Greek (*aster*) meaning "star." The species name comes from the Latin (*novus* and *anglia*) meaning "New England." Of the many asters that bloom during the late summer and autumn, this is the largest and most showy. When one closely observes the natural world, it can be learned that there is a strong interdependence between predator, prey, and wildflowers. In the proper sequence, called a food chain, each receives energy from the others. In this manner the individuals survive to reproduce and thus ensure the survival of the species. Native.

Range Widely distributed throughout the state.

Habitat Fields, thickets, and swamps.
Blooming Period August–October.

Crooked-stemmed Aster
(Aster prenanthoides)
Aster Family (Asteraceae)

Heart-leaved Aster
(Aster cordifolius)
Aster Family (Asteraceae)

Common Burdock
(Arctium minus)
Aster Family (Asteraceae)

Description Pale blue (or lavender) flower head, 1" wide, with 20–30 ray flowers. Disk yellow. Leaves narrow, with long-winged petioles, clasping the stem. Distinctive stem, smooth, and zigzag. Height: 1–3 ft.

Comments Perennial. Examine the stem to notice that the angle changes at each node where a clasping leaf is attached. The common name describes the stem of this aster, which is usually found growing in wet areas. Native.

Range Widely distributed throughout the state.

Habitat Streambanks, wet thickets, fields, and woodlands.

Blooming Period August–October.

Description Pale blue flowers, ⅝" wide, with 8–20 rays, growing in dense clusters. Disks yellow to reddish. Leaves alternate, sharply toothed. Petioles not winged. Stem smooth, many branches. Height: 1–4 ft.

Comments Perennial. The common name describes the shape of the leaves of this attractive fall aster. The genus name comes from Latin (*aster*) meaning "star." Like other asters, the flowers are pollinated by bees and wasps, especially yellowjackets, and the seeds provide food for many birds throughout the winter. The tiny seeds have white parachutes and are dispersed by the wind. All of Ohio's asters are perennials. Similar to Arrow-leaved Aster (*A. sagittifolius*), which has winged petioles. Native.

Range Throughout the state.

Habitat Dry woods, thickets, and clearings.

Blooming Period August–October.

Description Purple flower heads, ¾" wide, surrounded by tiny green, narrow, hooked bracts. Leaves alternate. Lower leaves 12–18" long, with hollow petioles. Stem smooth, grooved. Height: 3–5 ft.

Comments Biennial. Burdock produces a rosette of leaves 12" long the first year and an erect flowering stem the year following. With a hand lens, tiny hooks can be observed at the tips of the spines of the seed head (the bur). These hooks gave George de Mestral, a Swiss engineer, the idea for the invention of Velcro, which he patented in 1955. The name is derived from velvet (vel) and crochet (cro) from the French word for small hook. The prickly heads easily attach to animal fur and clothes, thus providing an excellent mechanism for seed dispersal. Introduced from Eurasia.

Range Naturalized throughout the state.

Habitat Old fields, barnyards, roadsides, and disturbed areas.

Blooming Period July–October.

Nodding Thistle
(Carduus nutans)
Aster Family (Asteraceae)

Bull Thistle
(Cirsium vulgare)
Aster Family (Asteraceae)

Canada Thistle
(Cirsium arvense)
Aster Family (Asteraceae)

Description Large, solitary purple flower, 1½–2" wide, at the top of a tall, drooping stem. Distinctive nodding head with large, reflexed purple bracts below. Leaves very spiny, with bases extending along the stem as prickly wings. Height: 3–6 ft.

Comments Biennial. Also known as Musk Thistle. Thistles are avoided by cattle, sheep, and goats, and therefore grow in great numbers in a pasture. Thistles are pollinated by butterflies, and the seeds are a favorite food of goldfinches. Introduced from Europe.

Range Widely scattered throughout the state.

Habitat Commonly occurring in calcareous soil. Fields, roadsides, and disturbed areas.

Blooming Period June–October.

Description Solitary purple flower head, 1–2" wide, at the ends of very prickly branches. Bracts spiny with distinctive yellow tips. Leaves coarsely pinnately lobed, spiny. Distinctive stem with prickly wings running downward from the leaves. Height: 3–6 ft.

Comments Biennial. Bull Thistle produces a rosette of leaves the first year and an erect flowering stem the year following. The featherlike "down" on the seeds is blown by the wind to distribute the seeds over long distances. Introduced from Europe.

Range Naturalized throughout the state.

Habitat Fields, roadsides, and waste places.

Blooming Period June–September.

Description Numerous, clustered, pale purple flower heads, ½–¾" wide. Leaves spiny and wavy edged. Stem hairless. Height: 1–5 ft.

Comments Perennial. This is our most common and widespread thistle. The species spreads rapidly and is difficult to eradicate because of extensive and deep roots. It is regarded as a serious weed in agriculture. Introduced from Europe.

Range Naturalized and locally abundant throughout the state.

Habitat Fields, gardens, roadsides, and other disturbed areas.

Blooming Period June–September.

Field Thistle
(Cirsium discolor)
Aster Family (Asteraceae)

Chicory
(Cichorium intybus)
Aster Family (Asteraceae)

Tall Blue Lettuce
(Lactuca floridana)
Aster Family (Asteraceae)

Cindy Tucci

Description Solitary, light purple flower head, 1–2" wide. Upper leaves embrace the flower head. Leaves alternate, deeply cut, with white woolly hairs on underside. Stem grooved, hairy, and without wings. Height: 3–7 ft.

Comments Perennial. The seeds provide important food for goldfinches. However, it is a troublesome weed for agriculture. It is similar to Bull Thistle (*C. vulgare*), which has spiny wings along the stem. Native.

Range Throughout the state.

Habitat Fields, woodland borders, and disturbed areas.

Blooming Period July–October.

Description Sky-blue flowers, 1½" wide, with petals toothed at the tips, stalkless, growing along the branches. The flowers bloom in the morning, wilt, and lose their color soon after midday. Stem much-branched, and nearly naked. Height: 1–4 ft.

Comments Perennial. Note the basal leaves which are toothed and dandelion-like. The root can be roasted, ground, and used in flavoring coffee, or even as a coffee substitute. It is related to the cultivated salad plant, endive (*C. endiva*). A mixture of Chicory and Queen Anne's Lace beautifies the highways in summer. Introduced from Europe.

Range Well established throughout the state.

Habitat Roadsides, fields, and other disturbed areas.

Blooming Period June–October.

Description Pale blue flowers, ½" wide, with 11–17 rays, in a loose cluster of 10–20 flower heads. Distinctive leaves deeply cut, dandelion-like. Height: 2–7 ft.

Comments Biennial. Wild Lettuce is related to garden lettuce. If garden lettuce were allowed to go to seed, the floral resemblance would be seen. The seeds are dispersed by means of parachutes which are carried long distances by the wind. Native.

Range Common throughout eastern and southern Ohio. Scattered northward.

Habitat Wet thickets, roadsides, woodland borders, and wooded floodplains.

Blooming Period July–September.

Green and Brown flowers

Common Cattail

(Typha latifolia)
Cattail Family (Typhaceae)

Narrow-leaved Cattail

(Typha angustifolia)
Cattail Family (Typhaceae)

Green Dragon

(Arisaema dracontium)
Arum Family (Araceae)

George Phinney

Description Minute brown flowers growing in dense spikes. The upper spike has staminate flowers, and the lower has pistillate flowers. The two spikes touch each other. Mature spike about 1" in diameter. Leaves 1" wide and nearly flat. Height: 3–9 ft.

Comments Perennial. Cattails are tall marsh plants that grow in dense stands in shallow water. A single seedhead contains about 250,000 seeds, each equipped with a tiny parachute that will carry it away in the wind. The rootstock, mostly starch, is edible. Native Americans and early settlers prepared flour from the crushed, dried roots. Cattails are popular for use in dried flower arrangements. Native.

Range Occurs in every county of the state.

Habitat Lake shores, marshes, pond edges, and wet ditches.

Blooming Period May–July.

Description Minute brown flowers in dense, cylindrical spikes. The upper spike has staminate flowers and produces pollen. The lower spike has pistillate flowers, and develops into the well-known cattail. The two spikes are separated by 1–2" of bare stalk. Leaves ½" wide and rounded on one side. A tall marsh plant. Height: 2–5 ft.

Comments Perennial. Cattails quickly colonize recently constructed artificial ponds and lakes. They are commonly introduced by migrating waterfowl. Patches of Cattails are favorite nesting sites for Red-winged Blackbirds. Muskrats feed regularly on the rootstocks. Narrow-leaved Cattails are more tolerant of alkaline soils than the Common Cattail (*T. latifolia*). It is common throughout the Eastern and Western hemispheres. Native.

Range Throughout the state.

Habitat Marshes, pond and lake margins, and wet ditches.

Blooming Period May–July.

Description Distinctive solitary green flower, 4–8" tall, with the spadix growing several inches above the spathe. Leaf solitary, divided into 5–15 leaflets. Stem smooth. Height: 1–4 ft.

Comments Perennial. The unusual shape of the flower is often said to resemble either the tongue or the tail of a dragon, hence the common name. Some people suggest it resembles the familiar northern constellation, Draco, the dragon. The species name comes from the Latin (*draco*) meaning "dragon." The mature fruit is a cluster of red berries. It is less common than its relative, Jack-in-the-pulpit (*A. triphyllum*). Native.

Range Throughout the state.

Habitat Moist soil of low, rich woods and streambanks.

Blooming Period May–June.

Tom Hissong

Cindy Tucci

Skunk Cabbage
(Symplocarpus foetidus)
Arum Family (Araceae)

Jack-in-the-pulpit
(Arisaema triphyllum)
Arum Family (Araceae)

Description Solitary green flower, often striped, 2–3" tall, with a hood arching over the club-shaped, flowering spike (spadix). "Jack" is the spadix, standing tall within the funnel-shaped spathe, or "pulpit." The plant is dioecious, meaning male and female flowers are produced on separate plants. Leaves with 3 leaflets, pale beneath. Mature fruit a cluster of scarlet berries. Height: 1–3 ft.

Comments Perennial. Also known as Indian Turnip. At first it may be overlooked because its green color blends in so closely with the other lush spring growth. The spadix releases a foul-smelling odor which attracts flies as the chief pollinators. The roots are full of hot-tasting calcium oxalate crystals that can blister sensitive skin. However, if sliced thin and thoroughly cooked, the root becomes edible. Native.

Range Common throughout most of the state.

Habitat Rich, moist woods.

Blooming Period April–June.

Description Brownish-purple and green, mottled shell-like hood (spathe), 3–6" tall, enclosing the knob-shaped flower cluster (spadix). Leaves coiled at time of flowering, later unfold into large cabbage-like leaves. However, it is not a true cabbage. Height of leaves at maturity: 1–2 ft.

Comments Perennial. This is the earliest wildflower to come into bloom, a forerunner of spring. The cellular activity that accompanies its rapid growth produces enough heat to melt any snow and ice from around the plant. The plant gives off the odor of decaying flesh (a foetid odor), which attracts insects that pollinate the flower. Native.

Range Scattered throughout the state.

Habitat Swamps, marshes, and very wet woods.

Blooming Period February–April.

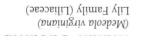

David Dister

Indian Cucumber-root
(*Medeola virginiana*)
Lily Family (Liliaceae)

Solomon's Seal
(*Polygonatum biflorum*)
Lily Family (Liliaceae)

Description Greenish flowers, ½" long, bell-shaped, usually in pairs, hanging beneath leaf axils along the unbranched stem. Leaves alternate, 2 times as long as wide. Berries blue to black (non-edible). Height: 1–3 ft.

Comments Perennial. Each year the leafy stalks die and leave a scar on the underground rootstock. These scars are said to resemble the official seal of Solomon, the king of Israel in the 10th century B.C. The starchy rootstock was a source of food for Native Americans and early settlers. Native.

Range Widespread throughout the state.
Habitat Dry to moist woods and thickets.
Blooming Period May–June.

Description Nodding greenish-yellow flowers, ½" wide, on a slender stalk. Petals and sepals curve backwards. Stamens red. Distinctive leaves in 2 whorls: 3–5 leaves at the top and 5–9 leaves near the middle of the stem. Berries dark purple. Stem erect. Height: 1–3 ft.

Comments Perennial. The flowers are so inconspicuous that they are often overlooked. Native Americans used the taproot, which tastes like a cucumber, for food. The plant is confined to old, stable forests and woodlands. Habitat destruction poses a serious threat to this unique wildflower. Native.

Range Mostly in eastern and southern counties; some scattered sites in northwestern counties.

Habitat Rich moist woods with deep, loose, slightly acid soil.

Blooming Period May–June.

Jeanne Willis

Large Twayblade
(Liparis liliifolia)
Orchid Family (Orchidaceae)

Wood Nettle
(Laportea canadensis)
Nettle Family (Urticaceae)

Description Purplish-brown flowers, ½" long, broad lip with purple veins, growing in a loose spike-like cluster. Leaves 2, glossy, oval, basal. Height: 4–10".

Comments Perennial. This member of the Orchid Family has a delicate appearance. It can be easily overlooked because it blends in so well with its environment. Like most orchids, they are largely dependent upon insects to aid in fertilization. This species will not survive transplanting and should remain in its existing location. Native.

Range Mostly in the eastern and southern counties of the state.

Habitat Rich woods, pine woods, thickets, and mossy banks of small streams.

Blooming Period May–July.

Description Tiny greenish flowers in spreading clusters, growing in leaf axils. Leaves alternate, arrow-shaped, and toothed. Leaves and stem densely covered with stinging hairs. Height: 1–4 ft.

Comments Perennial. *Caution: DO NOT TOUCH.* The entire plant is covered with stinging hairs that release an acid which causes a severe burning sensation to the bare skin. This is a chemical defense mechanism which discourages plant-eating mammals from eating and possibly eliminating the plant from its habitat. Similar to Stinging Nettle (*Urtica dioica*), which has opposite leaves. Native.

Range Throughout the state.

Habitat Moist woods, wooded floodplains, and stream margins.

Blooming Period July–September.

Early Meadow-rue
(Thalictrum dioicum)
Buttercup Family (Ranunculaceae)

Curled Dock
(Rumex crispus)
Buckwheat Family (Polygonaceae)

Wild Ginger
(Asarum canadense)
Birthwort Family (Aristolochiaceae)

Description Solitary maroon (to brown) cup-shaped flower, 1" wide. The flower is formed from 3 sepals with 3 sharply pointed spreading lobes. This solitary flower grows at ground level in the fork between 2 large, heart-shaped leaves. Height: 6–12".

Comments Perennial. The flower often goes unnoticed because it grows on the ground and is hidden beneath the handsome leaves. The roots have a ginger odor and taste, and when cooked with sugar can be used as a substitute for ginger spice. However, true ginger is derived from a tropical plant. Native.

Range Throughout the state.

Habitat Rich woods and wooded floodplains.

Blooming Period April–May.

Description Small green flowers, whorled in a tall cluster (raceme). Leaves narrow, with wavy and curled margins. Height: 1–4 ft.

Comments Perennial. The taproot can grow up to 6 ft. deep. Each year in the autumn, it grows new leaves in the form of a rosette. The seeds are brown and 3-winged. They remain on the stalk into winter. The seeds are eaten by many winter birds, including more than 20 species of ducks. Introduced from Europe, possibly as a common impurity of commercial seeds.

Range Naturalized and widespread through the state.

Habitat Moist fields, lake shores, roadsides, and disturbed areas.

Blooming Period May–September.

Description Small, greenish, drooping flowers, ¼" long, with 4–5 petal-like sepals. Leaves drooping, with 3 rounded lobes on long stalks. Height: 1–2 ft.

Comments Perennial. The species name comes from the Greek (*di* and *oikos*) meaning "two houses" in reference to the male and female flowers occurring on separate plants (dioecious). The male flowers have long, drooping yellow anthers, while the female flowers have fewer, drooping purple pistils. The flowers bloom in the early spring, just as the trees are beginning to leaf out. Native.

Range Throughout the state.

Habitat Moist, rich woods.

Blooming Period April–May.

Goldenseal
(Hydrastis canadensis)
Buttercup Family (Ranunculaceae)

Blue Cohosh
(Caulophyllum thalictroides)
Barberry Family (Berberidaceae)

American Columbo
(Swertia caroliniensis)
Gentian Family (Gentianaceae)

Description Solitary, terminal greenish (to white) flower, ½" wide, with numerous stamens and pistils. Petals absent. 3 leaves, deeply lobed: 2 stem leaves, 1 basal leaf. Rootstock thick, yellow. Height: 8–15".

Comments Perennial. Goldenseal has no petals and the sepals fall as the flower opens, producing a distinctive display of the numerous stamens and pistils. The fruit is a tight cluster of red berries. Native Americans and early settlers used the roots as a tonic, insect repellent, and yellow dye. More recently it was collected as the source of the drug hydrastine, used to inhibit uterine bleeding. The overcollection of the roots has contributed to its scarcity. Native.

Range Throughout the state.

Habitat Deep rich woods, wooded slopes, and shaded streambanks.

Blooming Period April–May.

Description Greenish-purple flower, ½" wide, with 6 sepals and 6 small gland-like petals. Flowers grow in a loosely branched terminal cluster. Leaves are divided into many leaflets. Height: 1–3 ft.

Comments Perennial. Also known as Papoose-root. The fruit is blue berry-like seeds. Native Americans and early settlers used the root for medicinal purposes to ease the pain of childbirth. Pollination is by bumblebees and other bees. The leaflets resemble those of Meadow Rue (*Thalictrum*), hence the species name *thalictroides*. Native.

Range Throughout eastern and southern Ohio. Less frequent in the northwestern counties.

Habitat Moist, rich woods, especially mixed hardwood forests.

Blooming Period April–May.

Description Greenish-yellow flowers, 1" wide, growing in large loose clusters up to 15" tall. Flowers have 4 petals lined with purple dots. Leaves in whorls of 4. Basal leaves up to 15" long. Stem stout. Height: 3–8 ft.

Comments A short-lived perennial. Some botanists describe it as a triennial plant: in the first year it produces a rosette of leaves, in the second year the rosette increases greatly in size, and in the third year the flower stalk grows and produces the spectacular cluster of flowers. Also known as Monument Plant because of its great height. It is named for the Dutch herbalist Emanuel Sweert, born in 1552. Native.

Range Mostly in the southern and a few northeastern counties of the state.

Habitat Dry open woods, meadows, and roadside banks.

Blooming Period June–July.

Squawroot
(Conopholis americana)
Broomrape Family (Orobanchaceae)

Giant Ragweed
(Ambrosia trifida)
Aster Family (Asteraceae)

Common Ragweed
(Ambrosia artemisiifolia)
Aster Family (Asteraceae)

Ken Hays

Description Overlapping brown scales, hiding pale yellow flowers. The leaf scales on the stalk overlap, thus somewhat resembling a long, narrow pine cone. No apparent leaves. Height: 3–10".

Comments The Broomrape Family is a small group of plants that completely lacks chlorophyll, thus they must become parasites on other plants for their nourishment. Squawroot is parasitic on the roots of hardwood trees, especially oaks. As we change the environment, we change the wildflowers. The survival of Squawroot depends on the preservation of old-growth woodlands. Native.

Range Throughout the state.
Habitat Rich oak woodlands.
Blooming Period April–June.

Description Tiny green flowers in spikes, 1–10" tall. Leaves large, opposite, and nearly always with 3 deep lobes. Stem rough and hairy. Height: 2–15 ft.

Comments Annual. This is the giant among the ragweeds. The pollen is spread by wind and is a principal cause of hay fever. Wind-pollinated plants tend to live in open, windswept areas. The flowers of wind-pollinated plants tend to be inconspicuous, and lacking in odor and color. Giant Ragweed is highly adaptive and quickly invades recently disturbed, moist areas. Native.

Range Common in every Ohio county.
Habitat Floodplains, roadside ditches, and other moist, disturbed areas.
Blooming Period July–October.

Description Tiny green flowers in spikes, 1–6" tall. Leaves highly dissected, fern-like. Stem hairy. Height: 1–6 ft.

Comments Annual. The common name describes the ragged appearance of the deeply divided leaves. The pollen is spread by wind and is a principal cause of hay fever. The oil-rich seeds are a valuable source of food for songbirds and upland game birds. The seeds can remain viable in the soil for many years. When conditions permit, the seeds germinate, the plant grows and reproduces very quickly in dry areas. Common Ragweed grows equally well in the city and countryside. Native.

Range Occurs in all Ohio counties.
Habitat Dry soil, fields, roadsides, and disturbed areas.
Blooming Period August–October.

BIBLIOGRAPHY

Andreas, Barbara K., *The Vascular Flora of the Glaciated Allegheny Plateau Region of Ohio.* Columbus: College of Biological Sciences, Ohio State University, 1989.

Braun, E. Lucy, *The Monocotyledoneae.* Columbus: Ohio State University Press, 1967.

Britton, Nathanial L., and Addison Brown, *An Illustrated Flora of the Northern United States and Canada.* 3 vols. 2d ed. New York: Dover, 1970.

Cooperrider, Tom S., *The Dicotyledoneae of Ohio. Part 2: Linaceae through Campanulaceae.* Columbus: Ohio State University Press, 1995.

Fernald, Merritt Lyndon, *Gray's Manual of Botany.* 8th ed. New York: American Book Company, 1950.

Fisher, R. Richard, *The Dicotyledoneae of Ohio. Part 3: Asteraceae.* Columbus: Ohio State University Press, 1988.

Gleason, Henry A., and Arthur Cronquist, *Manual of Vascular Plants of Northeastern United States and Adjacent Canada.* 2d ed. Bronx: New York Botanical Garden, 1991.

Grimm, William C., *The Illustrated Book of Wildflowers and Shrubs.* Harrisburg: Stackpole Books, 1993.

Headstrom, Richard, *Suburban Wildflowers.* Englewood Cliffs: Prentice-Hall, Inc., 1984.

Lund, Harry C., *Michigan Wildflowers.* West Bloomfield: Northmont Publishing, Inc., 1994.

Martin, Alexander C., *Weeds.* New York: Western Publishing Co., Inc., 1987.

Mathews, F. Schuyler, *Field Book of American Wild Flowers.* New York: G. P. Putnam's Sons, 1929.

Moseley, Richard E., Alvin E. Staffan, and Guy L. Denny, *Ohio Wildflowers.* Columbus: Ohio Department of Natural Resources, 1980.

Newcomb, Lawrence, *Newcomb's Wildflower Guide*. Boston-Toronto: Little, Brown and Co., 1977.

Niering, William A., and Nancy C. Olmstead, *National Audubon Society Field Guide to North American Wildflowers*. New York: Alfred A. Knopf, 1995.

Palmer, E. Laurence, and H. S. Fowler, *Fieldbook of Natural History*. New York: McGraw-Hill, 1975.

Peterson, Roger Tory, and Margaret McKenny, *A Field Guide to Wildflowers*. Boston: Houghton Mifflin, 1968.

Raven, Peter H., Ray F. Evert, and Helena Curtis, *Biology of Plants*. 3d ed. New York: Worth Publishers, Inc., 1981.

Rickett, Harold William, *The New Fieldbook of American Wildflowers*. New York: G. P. Putnam's Sons, 1963.

Venning, Frank D., *Wildflowers of North America*. New York: Golden Press, 1984.

Weishaupt, Clara G., *Vascular Plants of Ohio*. 3d ed. Dubuque: Kendall/Hunt, 1971.

Wharton, Mary E., and Roger W. Barbour, *Wildflowers & Ferns of Kentucky*. Lexington: University Press of Kentucky, 1979.

INDEX

BOB HENN has walked the trails of Ohio since the early 1950s. During these years he has led many field trips introducing countless numbers of youths and adults to wildflowers and to the role of wildflowers in the balance of nature. He has degrees from Otterbein College, Baylor University, and Miami University. Presently, he is Professor Emeritus in the Biology Department of Sinclair Community College, Dayton, Ohio.

—*Photo by Dave Henn*

A. Pizzino (440) 248-4583

Hepatica - march - april 15c

Boneset 50 - July - Oct

Goldenseal 202 2c
back path facing w on L